Praise 1

"What I truly appreciate about this book is that it not only focuses on tapping into your staff members' strengths and bringing out their best but it also provides ideas literally for every month of the year. You can pick up this book several times throughout the year or read it all at once and get great ideas to serve your staff. This is an easy read, packed with great ideas and strategies for purposeful leadership."

—**George Couros**, speaker and author of *The Innovator's Mindset* and coauthor of *Innovate Inside the Box*

"If school leaders are looking for ideas on how to show appreciation and lift campus morale, *Lead with Appreciation* is a great place to start! It's easy to read and more importantly, its ideas are easy to apply! Teamann and Miller help leaders at all levels recognize that culture isn't something you think about just once; it has to happen regularly. It's an ongoing process!"

—**Shawn Achor**, *New York Times* best-selling author of *Big Potential* and *The Happiness Advantage*

"In *Lead with Appreciation,* Amber and Melinda show us all how to love what we do and appreciate those who serve with us. They have taught me the importance of filling the buckets of my staff and why I should fill my own bucket as well. If you want to learn the keys to motivating and empowering your staff or developing relationships through service on a deeper level, you need to get this book immediately. I will be the first one in line!"

—**Salome Thomas-EL**, award-winning principal, speaker and coauthor of *Passionate Leadership*

"Amber Teamann and Melinda Miller are the best of the best. As we know, leadership is not an event, and this book helps infuse powerful concepts into daily actions and routines. They have compiled an incredibly useful guide to support leaders at all levels. *Lead with Appreciation* is full of helpful ideas, strategies, and techniques that can be put to use by anyone seeking to add appreciation and gratitude to their workplace. It's a road map that can be easily followed.

"*Lead with Appreciation* will demystify ways to show appreciation to your staff, making it easy to begin to create a culture of gratitude. Through their witty sharing of experiences and ideas, Amber and Melinda help leaders plan out acts of appreciation throughout the course of the school year that won't overburden an administrator or leadership team. Recognition of an educator's efforts allows you to share and show your team you recognize how hard they work and how much it is valued."

—Todd Whitaker, PhD, professor of educational leadership at the University of Missouri and author of *School Culture Rewired*

"This is the definitive guide on how to appreciate your people. Melinda Miller and Amber Teamann tackle the tension many leaders face: We want everyone on our team to feel valued, but we know each educator experiences appreciation differently. *Lead with Appreciation* will help take the guesswork out of building a school culture where everyone feels valued. This book is jam-packed with practical ideas to help you build relationships and trust and how to appreciate your people more effectively."

—Brad Gustafson, EdD, National Distinguished Principal and author of *Reclaiming Our Calling*

"Amber and Melinda have taken their knowledge of building a culture of care and appreciation and put it into a resource that every leader should own! *Lead with Appreciation* is a gift to school leaders looking for ways to support and encourage their staff throughout the year."

—**Jessica Cabeen**, principal, speaker, author of *Hacking Early Learning*, coauthor of *Balance Like A Pirate*

"Psychologically healthy schools begin with administrators that practice gratitude and invest in making their teachers feel valued throughout the school year. But how? New and veteran leaders alike will love this comprehensive treasure trove of strategies they can immediately use to transform campus culture. Readers will find Teamann and Miller's intentionality and enthusiasm energizing and refreshing. Witty and wise, these two leaders share thoughtful stories and advice that leave readers feeling connected and confident that they, too, can *Lead with Appreciation*."

—**Shari Halpin**, social-emotional learning specialist, Wylie ISD

"Everyone wants to be appreciated and the best way to accomplish this goal is to show that you care. Melinda Miller and Amber Teamann map out specific strategies that can be implemented immediately to build a positive school culture grounded in relationships."

—**Eric Sheninger**, educator, speaker, author of *Digital Leadership* and *Learning Transformed*

"Principals wear many hats, one of the most important hats being the big role of leading the culture of the school by finding ways to appreciate, build relationships, encourage, and empower others. Amber and Melinda have put together a goldmine of practical ideas in *Lead with Appreciation* to help you do just that."

—**Jessica Johnson**, principal and coauthor of *Balance Like a Pirate*

"I believe that a positive culture begins with fostering positive relationships. Intentionality, practicality, and sincerity are the most important foundations. *Leading with Appreciation* provides easy, meaningful, and compelling strategies to support the mission of appreciating staff. This step-by-step, month-by-month guide would be helpful for the new and experienced administrator."

—**David Vinson, PhD,** superintendent, Wylie ISD

"*Lead with Appreciation* puts action behind servant leadership theory. Far too often as leaders, we focus most of our energy on school improvement, student achievement, meeting the demands of central office, and making sure we are meeting the needs of our community. These are all important aspects of leadership, but this leaves little time or energy to think about how to meet the needs of the teachers and support staff who are in the trenches with us each day. This book gives so many tips, strategies, and ideas to get leaders started on this important work. I strongly encourage you to add this to your leadership library!"

—**Sanée Bell, EdD,** principal, speaker, author of *Be Excellent on Purpose: Intentional Strategies for Impactful Leadership*

"Many leadership books help readers reflect on why they got into this business. Some books help the reader with how to do the job. Rarely do you find a text that merges both so incredibly well. Miller and Teamann do an outstanding job of providing both the WHY and the HOW to lead a group, with appreciation at the core of every decision. Whether you have been in school leadership for one year or for 30 years, this text will become a go to resource in helping to provide an environment where everyone can do their best work and feel appreciated."

—**Dr. Joe Sanfelippo,** Superintendent, co-author Hacking Leadership

A **LEAD** Like a PIRATE Guide

LEAD with
APPRECIATION

Fostering a Culture of Gratitude

Amber Teamann & Melinda Miller

Lead with Appreciation

©2019 by Amber Teamann and Melinda Miller

This book is available at special discounts when purchased in quantity for use as premiums, promotions, fundraisers, or for educational use. For inquiries and details, contact the publisher at books@daveburgessconsulting.com.

Published by Dave Burgess Consulting, Inc.
San Diego, CA
DaveBurgessConsulting.com

Cover Design by Genesis Kohler
Editing and Interior Design by My Writers' Connection

Library of Congress Control Number: 2019949589
Paperback ISBN: 978-1-949595-81-9
Ebook ISBN: 978-1-949595-82-6

First Printing: October 2019

To our families, school communities, and professional learning networks: Thank you for helping us learn, lead, and love. We are better together!

CONTENTS

Encourage and Appreciate like a PIRATE

Passion

Praise helps to maintain passion. Praise your people. Finding and focusing on strengths allows your team to feel more successful.

Immersion

Throw yourself into positivity and intentional appreciation. Inspire your people. Zig Ziglar says, "People often say that motivation doesn't last. Well, neither does bathing—that's why we recommend it daily."

Rapport

Relationships. Relationships. Relationships. A positive climate doesn't just happen, and providing anything less than that should not be an option. Building rapport with your entire school community is the first step toward creating a shared vision for your students.

Ask and Analyze

Know what your staff needs to feel appreciated. Use SurveyMonkey.com or a Google form and ask them. This information is a gold mine. With one simple question, What can I do to show you that you are appreciated? you will have a road map of fun ideas for the whole year.

Transformation

Positive recognition and appreciation can transform the workplace. Even if you have to rely on visual reminders, checklists, or cell phone alerts, focusing on the positive can be transformational. Talk the walk, walk the talk.

Enthusiasm

Enjoy your job. Teachers want to work for people who love what they do.

FOREWORD

By Beth Houf & Shelley Burgess

I (Beth) remember it as if it were yesterday: I sat completely over-whelmed in the middle of a packed presentation room at my first principal conference. It was March of my first year as a principal, and I barely had my nose above water. Melinda Miller was front and center, and within one minute of listening to her share, I was completely hooked. Her positive attitude and practical strategies for leading people well inspired me beyond belief. She helped me define the type of principal I wanted to be.

Although it took me a few years to get the hang of social media, I finally caught on in the summer of 2014. Melinda was one of the very first people I followed. And through her I found another pow-erhouse principal, Amber Teamann. I watched as Amber relentlessly promoted the positive things happening on her campus and with her staff.

From the beginning, Facebook felt like a social media burden for me—so much drama and fakeness. That changed for me in December of 2017 when I joined the Principals Staff Appreciation and Motivation group led by Amber and Melinda. They help build a culture of gratitude within the group, and that culture extended to the schools we each led. We shared freely and often. We supported each other. My faith in Facebook was restored as I felt the power of a strong PLN (personal/professional learning network) at work.

The life of an educational leader can be a lonely road. Your task list multiplies daily, yet time seems diminished. It is essential that you have a strong network of support to celebrate the great things happening as well as get you through the rough moments. Shelley and I wrote *Lead Like a PIRATE* to do just that. We wanted to help support educators by sharing our stories and strategies. We wanted to be sure that no one felt as if she or he was alone. Our goal has been to set up systems of support through our PLN to empower leaders to take risks to ensure that school is an amazing place for both students and staff.

Since the book's release, it has been inspiring to watch our #LeadLAP crew grow. The examples and stories shared daily on our hashtag are so inspiring. What we have come to realize is that we are surrounded by greatness that needs a voice. One evening after our book was published, we started brainstorming how we could continue to support leaders but in a way that wasn't the norm. One thing we discussed was that leaders sometimes get overwhelmed by the amount of information that is being shared at what seems like lightning speed. How could we offer bite-size expertise for leaders so they could make an even bigger impact on their schools? The *Lead Like a PIRATE Guides* were born.

We are honored to have Melinda and Amber join our *Lead Like a PIRATE Guide* family with *Lead with Appreciation: Fostering a Culture of Gratitude*. This book is jammed packed with ideas to show your appreciation for those whom you serve. Although these are designed through the lens of a building principal, examples can easily be adapted from any role.

As we write in *Lead Like a PIRATE*, PIRATE leadership is about being the kinds of leaders we always wanted to be and creating the kinds of schools we dream of for kids. These leaders relentlessly search for ways to make school an amazing place. These leaders don't simply believe schools can be better; they *know* schools can be better and stop at nothing to make it happen. Amber and Melinda model this in all that they do each day.

We are proud to have them as part of the crew!

Our Stories

"I've learned that people will forget what you said, people will forget what you did, but people will never forget how you made them feel."

–Maya Angelou

Melinda Miller is the proud principal of Willard East Elementary in Willard, Missouri. An award-winning administrator, @mmiller7571 often posts on *The Principal Blog* and can also be found on its Facebook page. Melinda found value in social media more than ten years ago when it was new and scary. Since then she has helped hundreds of administrators and teachers discover the benefits of using social media platforms. Melinda has two beautiful daughters who keep her extra busy during this season of life. Offering humor and honesty when you need it the most, her motto is "If you're not having fun, you're doing it wrong."

Amber Teamann, @8amber8, is the proud principal of Whitt Elementary School in Wylie, Texas. An award-winning administrator, she blogs at *Technically Yours, Teamann* to share her leadership ideas, triumphs, and failures with thousands of educators. An educator since 2002, Amber is a former fourth-grade teacher and Title I technology facilitator. She has allowed her favorite quote, "The smartest person in the room is the room," to drive the way she leads. Blogging about her experience in the classroom and across school districts, Amber has forged lasting relationships to empower and encourage those around her. Having had the opportunity to speak and present across the nation, she is fortunate enough to be able to blend her passion with her career. Amber is the wife to a lucky fireman and mom to two girls who keep her on her toes. When she isn't chasing them around, she's tweeting, reading, or cheering on her favorite sports teams.

Introduction
This is Us

Alone we are smart. Together we are brilliant.

—Steven W. Anderson

We are stronger and better collectively
than we are individually.

—*Lead Like A Pirate*

Amber and I (Melinda) met on social media six years ago and had an immediate connection. We shared an understanding of the positive power of social media, and together we built a niche of school leaders using these platforms for the greater good. We were both passionate about sharing our school stories, personal stories, and professional stories with anyone and everyone who chose to participate.

We also looked for support and encouragement. Leadership can be a lonely place when you are the primary leader in your position.

It's hard to remember to fill someone else's bucket when you aren't intentionally reflecting on how to fill your own bucket. Amber and I became each other's bucket fillers. Once we had that support, we could focus on others and bringing out the best in our teams.

There are many facets of education, and we understand that. Appreciation and motivation are just two pieces of the gigantic puzzle of leadership. These pieces, however, are vital to completing the overall picture. They're also complex. For many of us, appreciation and motivation are both a strength and a weakness. Sometimes we can focus too much on one or the other. The key is finding a healthy balance—making your employees feel truly valued while also cultivating their talents and skills.

Driving home from a conference, I (Melinda) was listening to a podcast about Facebook groups. I may or may not have been driving while creating the Principal Staff Appreciation & Motivation group, but I couldn't help it! I just knew it would be a game changer for principals. Amber goes along with most of my harebrained ideas, so I invited her to participate. Keep in mind that I was traveling and had no idea how to set up a Facebook group or configure all the settings. As soon as she got the invite, she agreed the group would be a hit, and before we knew it, we had seven members!

This Principal Staff Appreciation & Motivation group was designed as an administrators-only forum. The main reason was that we wanted to be able to surprise our teachers. Our teachers follow us on social media—all platforms of social media! When I created *The Principal Blog* Facebook page, the first people to follow it were my teachers. I loved this. Amber showcases and posts shout-outs to her staff all the time on social media. We wanted a way to share great ideas on social media but still surprise our teachers. We also wanted our Facebook group to deal with a super-specific topic to ensure that the discussion would always stay on point. (There are tons of Facebook groups out there for principals. Stephanie McConnell has a great one—Principal Principles—and its more than eleven thousand members discuss all things general to administrators.)

This book is our way of sharing with you some of the fabulous ideas we've generated in the past few years. We will provide you with enough ideas for a full school year of appreciation. Some will be pretty elaborate ideas, while others will be quite simple. We urge you to filter all of these ideas through the lens of your school community and its unique needs and circumstances.

Here are some questions that you'll likely find yourself asking as you read this book:

- Does money grow on trees in Texas and Missouri? How do these people pay for all this stuff?
- My school has 150 staff members! How am I going to make 150 painted wood decorations?
- What if I go to all this work and no one thanks me? What if no one says anything?
- Who's going to help me with all this "appreciation"?

Don't worry—we're going to do our best to answer them all for you!

WHAT'S
YOUR STYLE?

There is tremendous value in getting to know the people you work with and the members of your team. Relationship building isn't just a cliché; it can be the difference between a team that works together and a team that is together to work. Before you can appreciate your team, you need to get to know them! I (Amber) learned quickly in my first year that there is no rushing relationships. It was in December that I realized that even though I had been there six WHOLE months, I still hadn't invested in real quality time with my people. I'd been in the building six months, but in actual conversations, experiences, or trust-building opportunities, it was just a handful with each teacher. I had not intentionally been going out of my way to get to know them on a personal level but simply interacting with them daily on a professional one.

New leaders, learn this from my mistake! When you are in a new position or role, it's easy to get caught up in your excitement and energy. You've been waiting for this chance, and now you're the leader! You're in charge! You get to make decisions and make changes! Your position precedes your person each time you walk into a room. When you speak, you speak as the leader, as the one in evaluative control.

One of the things my current district utilizes is the Gallup's Strengths Finder. The Clifton StrengthsFinder is an online assessment that helps individuals identify, understand, and maximize their strengths. This is incredibly powerful for me not only to know more about myself but also to learn more about the people I am surrounded by. The bulk of the staff I hadn't hired, but through the Gallup lens, I was able to immediately get a feel for what they contributed to our team.

All people have a unique combination of talents, knowledge, and skills—strengths—that they use in their daily lives to do their work, achieve their goals, and interact with others. Gallup has found that when people understand and apply their strengths, the effect on their lives and work is transformational. "Gallup analysis reveals that people who use their strengths every day are three times more likely to report having an excellent quality of life, six times more likely to be engaged at work, 8% more productive, and 15% less likely to quit their jobs." My number one Gallup strength is "activator." An activator wants action, wants to jump right in and make things happen. I have learned to guard my impulsive "let's" so others around me don't feel the pressure to move as quickly as I do. I also surround myself with people who have different strengths. From our teacher leadership teams to my amazing AP and counselor, we make decisions as a team. While I ultimately have autonomy to make decisions, "because I said so" is a terrible leadership strategy. Making sure our relationships are as balanced as possible allows decisions to be made confidently, clearly, and to be easily communicated. These connections matter in every situation and hopefully convey to our campus that we are invested in making the RIGHT decision, not just the easiest or the most convenient one.

Why does this matter in a book about appreciation? It matters because you can't rush relationships, and you can't rush getting to know people. A team is only as strong as its weakest link, and part of your responsibility is to build up all the links. By recognizing each of your team members and knowing what makes them tick, you find where and how you can build them up. Employees who feel appreciated are going to do more than what is expected. Employee engagement is the appreciative acknowledgment of a person or a team's efforts that exceed the expectations of their role or behaviors that benefit the success of the business. This can be done formally or informally as long as the employee feels valued. How they each feel valued, though, will vary. There are a variety of additional ways you get to know your people.

 **A team is only as strong as its weakest link, and part of your responsibility is to build up all the links.**

I've mentioned the Clifton's Strengths Finder. Another tool I have used with my team is the Enneagram. The enneagram is a personality typing system that consists of nine different types. Everyone is considered to be one single type, although one can have traits belonging to other ones. We all know effective leadership depends on self-awareness and self-management. This requires a willingness to look inside oneself, to listen to feedback, and to respond to the needs of each situation. As a leader, both your strengths and your weaknesses have a huge impact on your staff and amongst your teams. If you have an opportunity to do ANY sort of personality quizzes or even take the easy enneagram quiz, you'll have an opportunity to see a different way of looking at your team's strengths and weaknesses. This will, again, allow you to best meet the needs of your people.

> **Disclaimer:** Not all of your staff will feel appreciated by "gifts." For the life of me, I (Melinda) could not figure out why my teachers did not feel appreciated or loved. I was working nights and weekends on treats and cute little Pinterest tokens of appreciation. Then my superintendent mentioned he had read *The 5 Languages of Appreciation in the Workplace: Empowering Organizations by Encouraging People* by Gary Chapman and Paul White. I immediately downloaded the book on Audible and started listening every morning while getting ready for work. It's like the "love languages," only it is appropriate for a work environment.

Here are the 5 Languages of Appreciation at Work:

- Acts of Service
- Tangible Gifts
- Quality Time
- Words of Affirmation
- Physical Touch (Appropriate for Workplace)

After finishing the book, I knew it would be valuable for me to know my teachers' languages of appreciation at work. I purchased the survey for each staff member and sent it out before school started. I anxiously awaited their results. They completed the survey and then emailed me the results. There is a PowerPoint template that you use to enter all the results.

To say the results were surprising would be an understatement. My language of appreciation is "gifts." Buy me all the things! My least language of appreciation is "words of affirmation." Telling me "good job" or saying complimentary things to me about my work . . . in one ear out the other. Buy me things; I love you! I was not shocked by these results in my own survey; however, I felt awful. How shallow and insensitive is it to "need" material things to feel good about myself?

What made this even harder to swallow is that I am *the only one* on my staff whose primary language of appreciation is "gifts." There's the answer. The appreciation I was showing was not *their* primary language of appreciation. I'll pause here for you to guess what my staff's primary language of appreciation is . . . *quality time!* What do administrators have the least amount of? *Quality time!* Needless to say, I am re-evaluating what I do to show appreciation to my teachers.

What this boils down to is that there are a lot of ways to get to know your staff. You can choose whichever one you feel comfortable with, but we do think these are helpful ways to start as you lead. Our goal for this book is to help you find ways to appreciate, encourage, and empower others. The group that Melinda and I started on Facebook was the catalyst for this book. It was a group for administrators that allowed us to share creative and easy ways to show our appreciation for our staff. Its membership is now in the thousands, and we have learned so much from so many of you! We plan to share many of those ideas in this book, which is broken down through the calendar year with special attention paid to what we think of as the "Big Three." Those would be October and February—which Melinda affectionately refers to as the "armpits of the school year"— and the holiday season of December. Although we'll focus on those three months, any of our ideas can be used at any time during the year. Whether you come across a fantastic sale on cute sticky notes, are having a particularly low season, or just want to make some co-workers smile, using any of these ideas can help improve the climate of your campus, office, or team.

Conclusion

Regardless of your work love language, Gallup strengths, or enneagram number, we guarantee there are people on your team who don't think or react in the same way you do. Our goal is to provide you with easy-to-implement ideas to meet as many needs on your team as possible. Even if you aren't comfortable showing appreciation in this way, we believe you will be able to find an idea that will work for your leadership style. These efforts can be delegated, simplified, and expanded. Think of them as a starting place and then use your imagination! With employee appreciation, you're not only boosting performance and engagement but your employees' well-being and health.

Reflect on Your Climate

Leadership Treasure Hunt
(Find This)

Have you taken a survey or personality-type test? Do you know what your work love language is?

Navigating the Seas
(Think about This)

We typically give to others in the manner in which we like to receive. Now that you know what your natural inclination is, how can you purposefully and intentionally add other types of appreciation to your list?

Charting the Course
(Take Action)

Have your staff complete a similar survey to learn the language of each employee on your team.

Share your thoughts and ideas!
#LeadWithAppreciation

ENCOURAGEMENT MATTERS

Pirate leaders infuse enthusiasm into their work.
They bring it every day, and they are committed to
being on. They are the champions and cheerleaders
of their schools and champions and cheerleaders of
those who work and learn there.

—Lead Like a PIRATE

Your crew is essential to the survival of your
building and the success of your students.

—Lead Like a PIRATE

Educators are being asked to do more with increasingly fewer resources. Our plates are full, and people keep serving up ideas, initiatives, and strategies for how to do our jobs differently. Overworked and underpaid, most teachers spend their days trying to do what they signed up to do— grow learners, change lives, and make a difference. That has become more and more complicated with ever-changing curricula, home concerns, and dwindling public funding and support. A national debate on the appropriateness of public education has empowered everyone to have an opinion on what we do and how we do it. It can be exhausting. It is exhausting. As a leader, looking out across a team, a campus, or a district can be overwhelming. There are only so many hours in the day and only so many dollars in a budget. Melinda and I (Amber), however, have an idea about how to ease some of this turmoil.

When we connected on Voxer (an asynchronous messaging tool) six years ago, we instantly connected. Whether you want to think of us as eternal optimists or as people who just think we deserve to be happy when we come to work each day, we consider it our personal mission to engage our staff in a positive, supportive way. Please don't hear what I'm *not* saying. **There's more to this job than snacks and happy notes**. But that's the whole point! We. Change. Lives. This is not work for the faint of heart. Any given day could see a myriad of tasks and decisions. Opportunities are before us each and every day to change the trajectory of an employee's career or a student's life. There are so many incredibly difficult facets to your position, and . . . we're trying to take one piece off your plate. What we don't need is stressed out, burned out, overworked, and underappreciated teachers deciding on these things!

While no one wants to sit next to the crazy, eternally happy person at every meeting, there is something to be said for approaching those to-do lists and daily plans with a positive mindset. Gallup is a company that has invested both money and time in surveys across a section of adults across the country. Gallup conducted a well-being survey of more than 150 countries, generating responses from 98 percent of the world's population. The data from this survey was summarized in a book by Tom Rath, *Wellbeing: The Five Essential*

Elements. What I took away most from this book is the importance of leaders engaging their employees. Consider the following:

> The most disengaged group of workers we have ever studied are those who have a manager who is simply not paying attention. If your manager ignores you, there is a forty percent chance that you will be actively disengaged or filled with hostility about your job. If your manager is at least paying attention—even if he is focusing on your weaknesses—the chances of your being actively disengaged go down to twenty-two percent. But if your manager is primarily focusing on your strengths, the chance of your being actively disengaged is just 1 percent, or one in one hundred.

How can we, as educators, support our teams and ensure that they are engaged and feeling appreciated? The answer to that question is what this book is all about!

A thermostat sets the temperature in a building. As the administrator, you are the thermostat in charge of setting the temperature at your school. As author Todd Whitaker says in *What Great Principals Do Differently*, "When the principal sneezes, the whole school catches a cold." Encouragement means more when it comes from you. Advice means more when it comes from you. Evaluative comments? They mean more coming from you. Use that power for good. From the office staff to the janitor, you are the one who sets the temperature. While you are certainly allowed to have a bad day, you

As the administrator, you are the thermostat in charge of setting the temperature at your school.

don't have the luxury of showing your stress, your anger, or your own drama when you are trying to lead. If you panic, they will panic. If you are stressed, they will be stressed. If you show appreciation and make it a point to meet the needs of your staff, they will, in turn, do the same for students. (We hope!)

We have data to run, student growth to measure, and curriculum to make viable. There is no end to a strong instructional leader's duties. Then you have the managerial side. Time cards, budgets, compliance. You have a campus of parents to support, and on any given day, that can run the gamut from threats to tears—sometimes in the same meeting! I have 662 of the cutest, smartest Wolves in all the land, and the very best part of my day is when I get to interact with them. At the same time, it's my responsibility to grow and empower my staff. My teachers' development should and can be driven by the example I set for them, and I want my actions to challenge, inspire, and motivate.

Not everyone thinks like me. (Shocker!) It has taken my team years—not months, but years—to understand that I love to give. Large and small, it's how I show my appreciation. Thoughtful notes, snacks, and treats on a cart are all ways that I show them that I see all that they are doing and how very thankful I am for all of it. The trick comes in knowing who eats healthy, who eats vegan, who is gluten free, and so on. That takes time, my friends! There are a couple of different ways I get to know my staff better each year. You've heard about doing unto others as you would have them do unto you? This is more like doing unto others as they would do unto themselves!

Each year I have my staff complete a 3-2-1. I have used this with parents, students, and teachers. The setup is simple. I ask them to tell me three things they love about their job, two things they find challenging, and one personal tidbit they want me to know about them. The 3-2-1 has given me a glimpse of what they value about their chosen paths as well as a unique set of facts to reference as I interact with each of them throughout the year. Whether you change it up seasonally or by semester, giving teachers the opportunity to slow down and be reflective is highly effective. It has been a very important tool for me as a leader. I have found that while most leaders ask their teams to reflect periodically, being intentional about how we ask them to reflect also honors their strengths.

We also start out each year with a "My Favorite Things" form, which yields everything from shirt sizes to favorite hot and cold beverages. We keep them on file in the office, which allows me to quickly find out a fave and meet a need during what might be a rough day. I take a picture of these favorites and save them in the notes section of my phone.

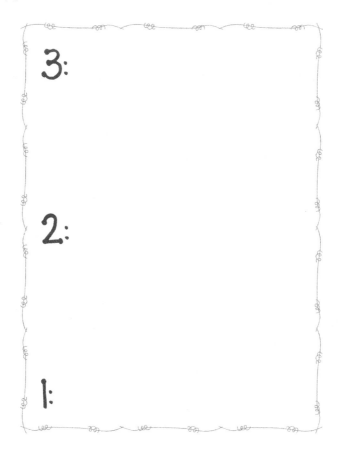

Controversial Amber strategy: I absolutely friend my teachers on Facebook. I don't ask them, but if they ask me, I absolutely say yes. This is an easy way to build relationships and be seen as Amber the person, not just the evaluative boss.

If a teacher posts about being up all night with a crying, sick baby, I want to meet that teacher at the door with grace and a latte. If I know a teacher is heading off for a family reunion because grandma is in poor health, I want to ask about grandma when that teacher returns. It's these little things that can make a world of difference to a teacher. To not take advantage of a tool that your students and families are already utilizing is missing a huge opportunity to truly connect. I don't ever want to miss an opportunity to say or do the little thing that can brighten someone's day.

FRIEND, FOE, OR STRONG LEADER?

Originally posted on amberteamann.com

Social media is everywhere. Between Twitter, Facebook, LinkedIn, Flickr, and more, not one facet of our lives has gone untouched by these unique platforms. President Barack Obama even utilized and took advantage of the generations that exist living in a world of status updates and constant awareness: 66 percent of young voters—those under the age of thirty—who voted in the 2008 election, voted for Barack Obama. Educators are held to a higher and different standard within society, and it stands to reason that the way we handle social media should be different. I go back and forth on my opinions and stances on this subject, leading me to believe that I might not really know what to think. I use Twitter for professional development (@8Amber8) and highly enjoy my PLN and all that it offers. It's a constant stream of new, different, and challenging that I am able to turn around and share with my peers. I use Facebook for my social *butterflyness*—my sorority sisters, high school classmates, and family. I also have several colleagues that are Facebook friends, and this is where the lines get blurry.

I have made it a point not to friend students. I work in an elementary school, so that isn't shocking. When I was teaching, I also made it a point not to friend my students' parents. As a principal, I have faced a new dilemma: Do I mix business with pleasure? I am "me" on Facebook. I post photos of my family, rant about my husband cutting baby wipes in half, and brag about my beautiful nieces and nephews. If I have a good day, I share. My sense of humor is my own, and I get all kinds of worked up during Dallas Cowboys games. At my first administrator-driven conference, I discussed with a group of my new peers about whether or not they friended their teachers on Facebook and while the answers varied, more erred on the side of no than yes.

After thinking this through and discussing it with several people I highly respect, I had to remind myself of the leader I want to be. I want to be approachable. I want to be seen as human, one who makes mistakes, and one who values relationships and people. I want to be real. One of my favorite people in the world made the comment that "relationships reduce rebellion." I think that is a gem of greatness. Enabling my staff to see me personally as well as professionally lets them see me transparently. I think it is an old-fashioned style of leadership that requires leaders to keep everyone at a safe and equal distance. Distance leads to a cold and sterile environment. That isn't what we want for our students, so why would we want it for our staff?

Professionally speaking, do you think it makes you a better leader if there is no connectivity between your personal life and your professional persona? Is it hard to respect someone you know IRL (in real life) if you're privy to what they think about a certain store or how their daughter did in soccer over the weekend?

Conclusion

It is important to lead in a way that is most comfortable to you. Assuming your staff members will appreciate and respond in the same manner as you, however, is the surest way to breed hostility. It might be easier to think of showing appreciation as a type of feedback, a way of increasing engagement and staff retention. Think of it as part of a larger process of building relationships, which might help frame the necessity of each idea we've presented. Appreciation is a powerful concept. It goes beyond praise, beyond positive reinforcement. Appreciation (or gratitude) is a recognition of our working together, of the fact that success is the result of team effort. Take advantage of social networks that allow you to make your campus or team stronger.

Reflect on Encouragement

Leadership Treasure Hunt
(Find This)

Find three new leaders to follow on a social media platform of your choice. Learn and borrow from the ideas and suggestions they share.

Navigating the Seas
(Think about This)

Think about the way you connect on social media. Are you choosing to let people see you?

Charting the Course
(Take Action)

Schedule three posts this week on a platform of your choice that showcase you and your pride in being a leader. It can be a quote, a praise, or a picture from something fun in your day. Just share!

Share your thoughts and ideas!
#LeadWithAppreciation

'I Need to Listen More Than I Talk'

It's easy to say that relationships matter. The tension (for me) comes from the fact that time is in short supply, and we all have a myriad of responsibilities that come with deadlines. The most effective school leaders I know understand how each individual they serve experiences their leadership differently. When we understand the unique needs of those around us, we are better equipped to meet their needs or empower them to do the same.

This is not a checklist endeavor that can be accomplished by planning the perfect office potluck or staff meeting. It's a daily discipline that works best when a leader is committed to listening, observing, and nurturing relationships with individuals (not just teams or a staff as a whole).

While these things are important, I've learned there are some things most teachers tend to appreciate.

- Educators want to feel supported.
- Educators want to know their time is valued.
- Educators want their strengths and ideas to matter.

When we're welcoming back our team each Fall, we minimize the number of meetings and maximize the time teachers have to prepare their classrooms. When we do meet during workshop week, we make sure the time is focused on only the things that matter most in the moment.

This past year, for example, we wanted to start the year in a positive and relational way while also sharing important information and updates. We rented a HUGE inflatable mini-golf course from a local rental company and set it up in our cafeteria the first day teachers reported back to work. We assigned every teacher to a golf foursome and made sure to include a new(er) staff member in each group. (These same golf-foursome groups were also used for collaborative cross-grade discussions at staff meetings later in the year.)

In addition to golfing together, teams interacted with some informational stations we had set up around the perimeter of the cafeteria. We rotated stations (and golf holes) every few minutes and managed to reconnect with one another while also learning key info to kick off the school year. The entire activity took a fraction of the time a typical workshop week "Welcome Back" session might take, and it was a blast!

We switch things up every school year, but the planning and changes are always informed by staff feedback and what individual teachers request. And what they typically request usually connects back to support, time, and valuing them as professionals.

These remain some of the truest forms of encouragement leaders can provide, but there's another aspect of encouragement that goes beyond what a person might request. Here's a story to explain what I mean:

I would not be the leader I am today without the encouragement of my first principal. I'll never forget the time she walked into my second-grade classroom and handed me a pamphlet while saying, "I think you'd be good at this." As it turned out, the pamphlet was for a university principal-licensure program.

This may sound crazy, but my first thought when I read the pamphlet was, *Am I not doing a good job as a teacher?*

After all, I thoroughly loved my job and was finally starting to feel a little competent. I had never considered serving as a school leader; in fact, if you had asked me back then what kind of encouragement I wanted, I would have told you that a simple acknowledgment of the innovative work our grade-level team was doing in mathematics instruction was more than enough encouragement for me.

My principal saw a strength in me that I never saw in myself, and I never would have asked for encouragement or a "push" in that direction. There's a difference between encourage-ment that supports us and encouragement that stretches us, and both are important.

Understanding the difference between these two types of encouragement (and who on your team is needing which type and when) can make or break the morale of a staff. When we are genuinely interested in another person's ability to thrive, we will take time to notice the things they'd like us to notice and illuminate what we see as a possible next step in their journey of becoming.

Be sure you're balancing encouragement that celebrates your people with encouragement that increases their capac-ity or vision.

—Brad Gustafson

LEARN
TO DELEGATE

**You can do anything, but you
can't do everything.**

–David Allen

**Success comes from delegating,
risk taking, and having a good team.**

– Richard Branson

There is no possible way that leaders can do #allthethings by themselves. It's simply not possible. Nor is it much fun when you try to go it alone. Everyone needs a team, and this chapter is dedicated to helping you gather yours, set some goals, and delegate the logistics that are vital to bringing it all together. We have a boatload of ideas, and we love all of them, but we want them to be manageable. We want them to be easy to implement and share with others—especially if you aren't inclined to think this way!

Everyone has strengths, but with all that you have on your administrative plate, it's easy to forget some of the "froufrou" stuff. We mentioned earlier how important it is to show appreciation and what a culture of appreciation can do for your employees. No matter how many years you have been on the job, whether it's five or fifteen, we believe there will be something in this book that feels genuine and allows you to express how much you appreciate your people!

Before you get started, take stock of your team—those people who will be working alongside you to put your appreciation into action. Along the way, you will likely question how you are going to get it all done and still keep the ship afloat, but with the right crew, you will survive. There are all different kinds of administrative teams. I (Melinda) have an assistant principal, a secretary, and a counselor, and I know I can share my crazy ideas with them at any given moment. If you don't have a team like this, identify someone or several someones who can help out. Culture is not only a leader's responsibility—everyone can play a role. Secretaries and assistants make great partners in crime because they know all the ways that your budget can be stretched.

Keep in mind that you can't (and shouldn't!) try to implement all of the ideas we will share in this book. Spread them out. Save some for next year and the year after that. You don't want the ideas to get stale or be taken for granted. We highly recommend pacing yourself!

Here are a few more tips to consider as you embark on your journey of appreciation:

Know your purpose.

At the beginning of every school year, I share a simple message with my office staff. I tell them that it's our job to take away the obstacles facing our faculty so they can focus solely on their classes and teaching during the school day. They will celebrate and appreciate our children, but we must celebrate and appreciate them as professionals. Our faculty members don't expect to be celebrated and appreciated, but the jobs they do and the dedication they have always improves when others notice.

Engage your parents.

Start by sharing your vision with your PTA (or PTO) leaders. The more helpers you have, the greater the division of labor. Ask general classroom parents to help. Like everyone else, they're busy, but many would love the opportunity to show their appreciation to their children's teachers. You might even consider involving some of your most challenging parents. Giving them an opportunity to contribute or have influence on some of the more meaningful, positive interactions is a great way to draw them in!

Engage your community.

Look beyond your school walls to the surrounding community. When it comes to showing appreciation, businesses and churches are often quite willing to make donations, volunteer, and sponsor events. We've asked local restaurants to donate chips and salsa from their menus. Local bakeries and mom-and-pop donut shops all become opportunities for contributions to your campus. You can reach out with a call or with an official letter on school letterhead. I always include the size of my campus and the reach of our social media to local businesses. Something to consider when reaching out to a business is how you can reciprocate the gesture. Giving that business a shout-out on your social media channels is a gesture that can bring that business more customers. Another idea is sending a thank-you picture or note from students. Some businesses will post these where all their customers can see it.

Recruit your family.

I use the term "recruit" lightly. My children don't really have a choice, and my mom understands it takes a village. They actually enjoy it. You will find that it is very rewarding for all your helpers. Showing appreciation for others fills your emotional bank account just as much as theirs and sometimes even more.

Include your teachers.

Teachers want to be included. Target some of your most creative educators—the ones who truly enjoy decorating, writing cute notes, and delivering special treats and can follow your vision—and you'll have a stellar team! Do you have a dedicated leadership team? We have an action team that has taken on improving culture, and some of the tokens of appreciation have been shifted to that group. We have also noticed that a lot of those teacher-leaders request access to our Facebook group. We made the decision early on that we didn't want to include them in that space so that we could have a safe place for administrators to speak, but there are social media platforms where ideas can be shared.

Include your students.

Don't forget your student body! What better way to teach empathy and gratitude than using a student leadership group? Maybe you have a student council. Even if you don't have an organized group of student leaders, students would love working on some of the projects and surprises shared in this book. Before school, after school, during lunch, during recess—no time is off limits when it comes to celebrating your staff!

Stay organized.

As far as keeping up with all these ideas and tasks, I do a couple things to ensure that we have a regularly occurring appreciation schedule. (I know that might sound artificial, but if it's important to you, you make a plan for it!) I don't know about you, but I have checklists for my checklists. From packing to meal planning, I have a list of what needs to happen to make it happen. Acts of appreciation are no different! Create a system that works for you. You can store your ideas in file folders with monthly labels or in a binder with tabs for each month. Another option is to create a template in Google Drive that your team has access to so everyone can see what is happening next.

Know your budget.

After assembling your mini appreciation army, you will start to wonder how you are going to pay for everything. Some things you will have to purchase, but you can pinch pennies by being resourceful!

Find out from your direct supervisor what your district policies or guidelines are when buying food and gifts. There might be a policy requiring that all food must be purchased from your district's food service program. Gift certificates are usually frowned upon by auditors. One idea that I (Melinda) use to give some freedoms for teachers is giving away a twenty-five-dollar "gift certificate" to a vendor that I know has been approved; for example, I award these paper gift certificates to Amazon, which just means the teacher gets to shop for and choose twenty-five dollars' worth of items of their choice. It's a fun gift but keeps me within my rules and guidelines, as we are allowed to shop from Amazon.

It's also important to recognize that not all of these things have to cost money. You can choose only those things that use paper or take time. There will be enough ideas that you could fill up a year's calendar without spending a dime.

We have used Signup.com to get parents to "Stock the Fridge" at the beginning of the year. (There is a list of items that can fill up the fridge that teachers use for snacks and drinks. They come and go as they please.) We chose that online tool because of the reminder emails that are sent straight from within the program. You can use a Google form or other tools as long as you remember to send the reminders. Reminders are key. Work with your PTA or PTO to determine which fundraiser dollars could be used for your appreciation projects. We've partnered with our school's "cheer fund" to help pay for special celebrations, such as National Popcorn Day and National Waffle Day.

Every school and district is different. There are amazing principals posting incredible things all over the internet. Things that can make you go oooh and ahhh. Principal Pinterest pressure is a real thing! Just remember that you don't know what's happening behind their highlight reel. It might be a small school with few staff members, or maybe it's a high socioeconomic district that raises thousands of dollars at bingo events where alcohol is served. It all goes back to your resourcefulness and your planning team's creativity. The bottom line is that you get to decide what you want and what your team needs, because as the leader, you know them best! Some campuses dress up for every holiday or weather change, and I happen to know that my staff would kill me if I made them do that! You get to do you!

Conclusion

There's a difference between being involved and being essential. Involving others and learning the leadership lesson of delegation will allow you to be productive and not just busy. Leverage the strengths of those around you, from your secretary's financial finesse to the former cheerleader on your team who can make amazing banners. There is nothing gained by assuming you are the only one allowed to shape your school's culture and show appreciation. Your influence comes from your guidance of your team's ideas, actions, and thoughts, not you getting it done all by yourself. The most effective leaders build the capacity of those around them.

REFLECT ON DELEGATION

Leadership Treasure Hunt (Find This)

Who are the members of your team you can include as a part of your appreciation team?

Navigating the Seas (Think about This)

What are the guiding principles you want your team to know when it comes to your campus vision of appreciation?

Charting the Course (Take Action)

Create a monthly to-do list, making sure to store it in file folders, a binder, or Google Drive for team members to access.

Share your thoughts and ideas!
#LeadWithAppreciation

SUMMER PREP

Be intentional about developing and
appreciation for what you see.

—Lead Like a PIRATE

The key is not to prioritize what's on your
schedule, but to schedule your priorities.

—Stephen Covey

Intentional time and focus devoted
to the right things are what will
ultimately propel you forward.

—Lead Like a PIRATE

Principal Matt Arend of Sigler Elementary School in Plano, Texas, sends his staff home each year with a Summer Selfie Bingo Challenge. He writes about this challenge on his blog, matthewarend.com, and you can read the entire post at bit.ly/leadWA1. What I like best is how he closes that post with "Yes, summer is meant to relax, unplug, reflect, and recharge, but while you are doing all of those important things, do not forget you are also building school culture. You have a lifestyle to create in your building. What are you waiting for?"

A lifestyle, a culture—that's the purpose of all of these activities, not cheesy trinkets or just another task on your to-do list. These are authentic ways to build and nurture your school's culture of appreciation and motivation even during the summer.

If you're like us, you know that the heavy lifting for the next school year begins as soon as the current year ends. When all the students have gone home, and your staff has started the summer, you finally have time to sit down, reflect, and start making plans. The calm and quiet of the summer can be a startling change from those fast-paced days of the school year, but if you do it right, the summer can be a time when you can develop a plan that ensures all of your great ideas actually take place!

One of the first things I do is make a list of all the school campus events that I know are going to happen. These are the events that happen each year regardless of my plan or schedule. I flip through my planner and make notes of all the things we've done in the past year and evaluate whether or not we are going to do them again. I add the ones that we'll continue doing to the pages of next year's planner. I also try to make sure I have at least one appreciation activity a month that's ready to roll even before the school year starts. This helps me balance anything else that comes my way throughout the course of the year.

By doing this in the summer, I am able to take the big-picture approach with my budget and know that in the craziness of October or May, I already have something lined up to celebrate our staff. I invite my assistant principal, secretary, and counselor to come in and discuss ideas. Each month has an easy "holiday," but it's the theme, idea, or cutesy part that we come up with in the summer that gives us a launching point. If you're not an on-the-spot thinker when it comes to gifts or acts of appreciation, the summer can be your key to success. We suggest taking notes from each chapter of this book and jotting them down in months in which you want to try and incorporate them. Choose one or two ideas you'd like to make happen during each month. Decide what you need to make it happen—budget, manpower, time—and work from there. I try to work one month ahead. My secretary knows when she has to go to the store well in advance and knows exactly what she needs. Working ahead allows you to feel confident that no matter what might pop up, you have a system in place for showing appreciation. If you come across a fabulous, last-minute idea, you can always add it. Be intentional. Don't wait till you feel like showing appreciation—make a plan for it! This timeline allows me to create any visuals I want to incorporate. There are a variety of ways to create social media images; you just have to find the one that fits you and your tech comfort level.

CREATING SOCIAL MEDIA IMAGES

Have you ever wondered how to create those perfect social media images that you see shared online? The ones with the great fonts and the perfectly apropos pictures that seem tailored to the campus message? Have no fear! The amazing Jessica Travis, kinder teacher, TPT superstar, and blogger at *Jessica Travis Teaching* shares with us her tips and tricks on creating the perfect image. The following was shared on her blog, *Jessica Travis Teaching,* on the post titled "Tech Tips With Travis: Creating A Social Media Image" (bit.ly/leadWA2).

Now there are ways that you can create these images on your phone . . . but for me, I create them on my home PC or laptop because that is where I have all of my clipart and fonts that I can use to create an image!

Step 1

You will need PowerPoint. Yep . . . that simple little program is what I create *everything* in . . .

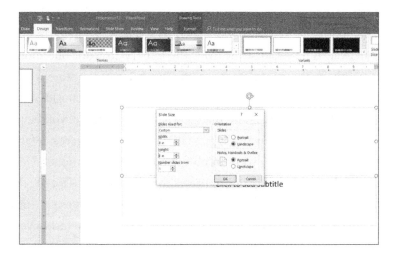

- Open PowerPoint and you are going to need to resize your slide. This is easy . . . simply click on the "design" tab. Locate "slide size" and you will have options as standard, widescreen, or customize. Click on "Customize."

- You will see this little box pop up! You will need to go in and manually change the width and height to 8 inches. This will create the perfect social media square!

  Note: For those of you that create on Teachers Pay Teachers and you see teachers with the perfect square covers to showcase their product . . .this is the size for that too!

- After resizing your slide to 8x8. Click "OK." You may be prompted with another sizing screen . . . Click on "Maximize."

Step 2

Now is the FUN part! You get to create whatever image you want! Some people still use the text box feature . . . but it drives me completely *insane*. Soooooo . . . I use the *"insert shape"* feature when I put text onto my slides.

- Click on "insert shape" and I usually choose the rectangle. It's just simple!)

- Place the shape on the screen where you wish . . . and type.

  Note: If for some reason it won't let you type—right click and click "edit text."

- Your text will appear white. Simply highlight the text and change the color to what you wish. (I wrote "type here" as an example—your screen will still appear blank until you type in the shape box.)

- While the blue filled box is a pretty shade of BLAH . . . I want JUST the text to appear with no background color! Soooooo . . . I change my font to black, and then I need to get the shape transparent!

- To do this: right click on your shape with text. Click on "Format Shape." You will need to click on "No Fill" under the fill section and "No Line" under the line section. Then click "OK" or "Apply."

  Note: You will want text in your shape box *before* making it transparent—many PowerPoint programs will delete the box if you do it prior to entering text.

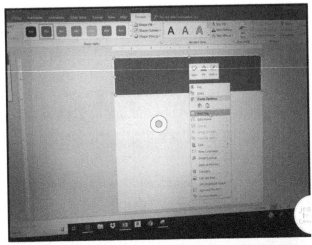

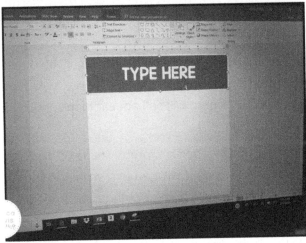

STEP 3: Design away!

You can easily move the shape of text where you need it.

To create another text shape box—*do not* go through all of those steps again. Simply click on the shape box, copy, and paste! *Voilà!* You now have a new box with text to move where you please on your 8×8 perfect slide.

You can insert clipart, pictures, or continue with the text that you need.

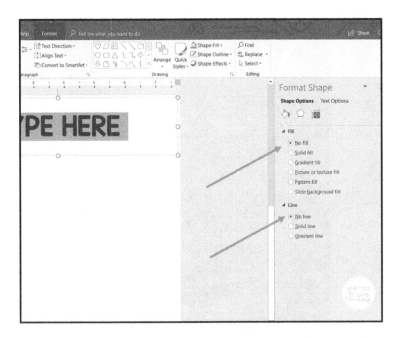

Simply click on "Insert Picture." Select a file from where you have saved an image.

But . . . then your picture is all *wonky* and on top of other pictures and images . . . something like this:

Don't worry! This is simple to fix.

Click on the image you want to move backward or forward. In this case, I am clicking on the little iPad to move behind the computer image.

Click on "Format" (The "Format" option will not be shown unless you have clicked on an image or box with text.)

You will see two options that say "Move Forward" or "Send

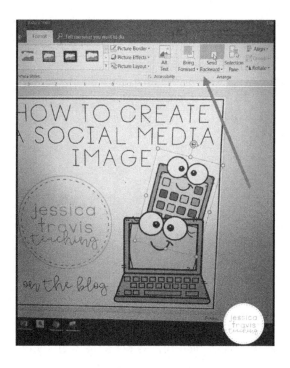

Backward." In this case, I want the iPad image to be sent backward behind the computer image. Click on the choice you want. (*You may have to click multiple times depending on the order in which you inserted the images!*).

Then . . . voilà . . . you have an image!

STEP 4: Saving your image.

To save this image for you to use in social media . . . there are two ways you can do this.

- **Option 1:** You can hit CTRL + A—this will highlight *everything* on your slide. After hitting CTRL + A (*at the same time*)—then right-click. You will find "Save as Picture" and click on that. This will bring up your tab that will allow you to save this image where needed (on your desktop, flash drive, etc.).

- **Option 2:** Find your Snipping Tool. (Use your start or search bar and type in "snipping tool.") It will bring up a little box—click on "New."

Using your mouse, you will click where to start and hold down to drag around the entire image. Once you have snipped it the way you want to save it . . . it comes up in a box that will allow you to "Save" or re-do by clicking "New" again.

Once you have it saved . . . you can email yourself the picture so that you have it for easy access on your phone (if that is how you insert images to your social media most often!), or you can simply insert it from your computer! If you choose to email it . . . simply open up your email and "Screenshot" the image.

Don't worry . . . it will still fit perfectly into your social media box (on Instagram) or simply edit if using Facebook from your phone!

When you insert it . . . it will be the *perfect* image! While this may seem like *a lot* of steps . . . have no fear! Once you play around with it a few times and insert your text shapes and images to create your design . . . it will come easy!

Who doesn't like to be told that she or he is doing something right and that their work is not going unnoticed?

Seasonal treats are easy and follow a calendar. These will give you a baseline of thoughtful giving, and then all the things you can additionally supplement along the way will just increase the atmosphere of appreciation. When you are appreciating like a pirate, you are intentional; you are immersing your people in a culture of appreciation. This means you know that by planning ahead, you remove the chance that during a busy stretch or stressful season, you don't lose sight of the fact that you are the one who sets the tone in your building. You want the tone to be one of appreciation.

Happy notes are a big way I meet my teachers' needs, especially those who have words of affirmation as their love language. I've designed two sets of happy notes that are easy to print and cut and have available for when you need them. As an educator, I (Amber) can tell you that I love receiving little notes of appreciation from my administrators and students every once in a while. Who doesn't like to be told that she or he is doing something right and that their work is not going unnoticed? Being an adult, let alone a child, can be really tough, so a little message to tell people that they are an important part of your day can go a long way! Thank-you notes! I created these half-sheet notes in an attempt to make sharing a "happy note" with my team easier. These small interactions can make a big difference in the day-to-day stressors of your team whether they be big or small. Print them out, in black and white or color, and have them cut and ready to go.

Thank-you notes or any style of words of affirmation or written praise for your team is also healthy! Various studies have found that

when people express what they're grateful for, their overall mood improves, and their depressive symptoms subside. They feel more at ease, less stressed, and more mindful of the things that make them happy—which, after writing the thank-you notes, can itself be added to the list. From *How Full Is Your Bucket?* by Tom Raft and Donald Clifton, the number one reason people leave their jobs is because they "do not feel appreciated." They also shared that people who feel appreciated or show praise and recognition:

- Exhibit increased productivity
- Are more engaged with their colleagues
- Are less likely to leave their current role
- Have higher rated feedback from their clientele (or customers)

How does that translate to education? You've heard that someone who feels appreciated will always do more than expected. I've mentioned before that I keep track of when and how I share praise on my team. (It is just a checklist with checks by a name each time I write a note.) In the same manner that I keep track of whom I send Christmas cards to, I keep a list of those whom I've celebrated or recognized.

Someone who feels appreciated will always do more than expected.

Someone once suggested that my praise was disingenuous because I track it, but if Gallup is correct, the majority of us don't give or receive anywhere near the amount of praise that we should. As a result, we're much less productive, and in many cases, completely disengaged in our jobs.

Ensuring that our team feels appreciated is a priority, and as the leader, it's my number one priority. Summer also gives you time to flesh out a theme if you're going to use one for the next year. A campus-level theme can be centered around a slogan, a vision, or even a book that we are going to read. That theme can be incorporated into your monthly treats or just be an aside.

- One year I purchased 4x6 frames from Amazon for each member of our staff. During the summer, I created quotes via PowerPoint that I could hand out each month. These were simple, but they all aligned with some gem of greatness that I wanted to share. These were easy to print out and place in their boxes each month. Having them all printed out and available also meant that I could pick and choose as needed if I knew a teacher was having a stressful day.

- How do you notify your teachers about upcoming events like back-to-school, professional development? Send them a themed invitation. Throw in some confetti or glitter, getting them excited about the upcoming year.

	A	B	C	D	E	F	G	H	I

Aldrich, Jennifer	☐	Leech, Tiffany	☐
Arellano, Denise	☐	Matthews, Autumn	☐
Boatman, Steve	☐	McKenna, Patricia	☐
Boruk, Lacey	☐	McReynolds, Shanda	☐
Braun, Kristin	☐	Meissner, Laura	☐
Bray, Laurissa	☐	Meyer, Joanna	☐
Brown, Brittney	☐	Nohrenberg, Debbie	☐
Brown, Jill	☐	Padden, Renee	☐
Burnett, Teri	☐	Palmer, Sharla	☐
Clark, Angela	☐	Paramore, Kristi	☐
Corso, Kim	☐	Patsy, Marlea	☐
Crim, Staci	☐	Power, Morgan	☐
Filip, Sarah	☐	Quagliarello, Kristi	☐
Frame, Michelle	☐	Richardson, Janet	☐
Galennie, Tracie	☐	Riley, Amy	☐
Gayken, Harley	☐	Rogers, Sherri	☐
Grant, Dawn	☐	Rowell, Dyann	☐
Halpin, Shari	☐	Schoeck, Marisol	☐
Hamm, Rebecca	☐	Seale, Stephanie	☐
Hauenstein, Debbie	☐	Shahan, Patricia	☐
Hunter, Jennifer	☐	Stevens, Kristin	☐
Jackson, Anita	☐	Suttle, Nancy	☐
Jacobs, Erin	☐	Teamann, Amber	☐
Jennings, Andrea	☐	Travis, Jessica	☐
Johnson, Jillo	☐	Turner, Emily	☐
Kendrick, Lisa	☐	Turner, Sheree	☐
Knapp, Kippy	☐	Wade, Allen	☐
Kuehnhold, Brittany	☐	Williams, Kristi	☐
Lack, Heather	☐		

Aldrich, Jennifer	☐	Leech, Tiffany	☐
Arellano, Denise	☐	Matthews, Autumn	☐
Boatman, Steve	☐	McKenna, Patricia	☐
Boruk, Lacey	☐	McReynolds, Shanda	☐
Braun, Kristin	☐	Meissner, Laura	☐
Bray, Laurissa	☐	Meyer, Joanna	☐
Brown, Brittney	☐	Nohrenberg, Debbie	☐
Brown, Jill	☐	Padden, Renee	☐
Burnett, Teri	☐	Palmer, Sharla	☐
Clark, Angela	☐	Paramore, Kristi	☐
Corso, Kim	☐	Patsy, Marlea	☐
Crim, Staci	☐	Power, Morgan	☐
Filip, Sarah	☐	Quagliarello, Kristi	☐
Frame, Michelle	☐	Richardson, Janet	☐
Galennie, Tracie	☐	Riley, Amy	☐
Gayken, Harley	☐	Rogers, Sherri	☐
Grant, Dawn	☐	Rowell, Dyann	☐
Halpin, Shari	☐	Schoeck, Marisol	☐
Hamm, Rebecca	☐	Seale, Stephanie	☐
Hauenstein, Debbie	☐	Shahan, Patricia	☐
Hunter, Jennifer	☐	Stevens, Kristin	☐
Jackson, Anita	☐	Suttle, Nancy	☐
Jacobs, Erin	☐	Teamann, Amber	☐
Jennings, Andrea	☐	Travis, Jessica	☐
Johnson, Jillo	☐	Turner, Emily	☐
Kendrick, Lisa	☐	Turner, Sheree	☐
Knapp, Kippy	☐	Wade, Allen	☐
Kuehnhold, Brittany	☐	Williams, Kristi	☐
Lack, Heather	☐		

#Take Control
It's your game!

#Take Control
It's your game!

WHITT ElemenTARY 2018-2019   **WHITT ElemenTARY 2018-2019**

- Mail your teachers a postcard during the summer months. You can thank them for the previous year, get them excited about the next year's theme, or just say you're checking in.
- Develop a music playlist to play as teachers enter the building on the first day back. It can be their favorite songs, songs that go with your theme, or dance party songs.
- Create your favorite-things list for teachers to complete when they come back. Although it may ask all the same questions, you can design it to fit your theme each year.

- Search sales for items that may lend themselves to your upcoming theme or ideas that correlate to your monthly ideas. Michaels, Hobby Lobby, Walmart—you never know what you'll find on clearance! I look for things that I can hand out to my leadership team, my office staff, or to my PTA board when an opportunity arises.

- Worried about money? Start a chain reaction! It can just be a bucket or box of "sunshine" or have a theme, and it can start with you and be refilled by staff members. Have a bucket system where you add items to share appreciation for each month of the school year. If a bucket is empty, you know you need to add something. Even if it's just cards with possibilities or suggestions, lining up the buckets is a great visual of the actions you plan on taking throughout the year.

Conclusion

Take advantage of the summer months. You typically have fewer interruptions and can make a year-at-a-glance kind of plan. Planning is essential to keep my mind ahead. Prioritizing ruthlessly seems to be the only way to accomplish what's most important in the little time we have. Prioritizing appreciation during your down months allows you to have some solid ideas at the heart of what you're going to do. When the craziness of October kicks in, if you see something fun or easy, it's a bonus, not an aside.

REFLECT ON SUMMER PREP

Leadership Treasure Hunt
(Find This)

Have a theme? Want a theme? Talk to your leadership
team and decide how thoroughly you want it integrated
for your campus. Map out a school year plan.

Navigating the Seas
(Think about This)

Think about how you like to be appreciated. Do
you have activities planned that speak to
a variety of styles and not just your own?

Charting the Course
(Take Action)

Create a have-a-happy-summer post
using Jessica Travis's tips above
(or through an app of your choice)!

Share your thoughts and ideas!
#LeadWithAppreciation

Empowering Others to Lead

I've been at the principal thing for about twelve years now, with five years of assistant principal experience and twelve years of teaching experience before that. That's twenty-nine years of experience as an educator. The one thing I can share is that tomorrow I will see something in our school that I have never seen before. That's the joy of education for me. One thing I've learned, though, is that I can't do this principal thing on my own. I don't have an assistant principal by title, but I do have a multitude of assistant principals that help me with decisions every single day.

Not having an assistant principal is actually a joke with a middle school Voxer group that I'm in. This group is amazing, and most of them are lucky to have an assistant principal or two. I feel very fortunate that our staff take on the roles of assistant principal. With so many assistant principals, I get a variety of thoughts and solutions to concerns that are brought my way. I've also learned that I need to listen more than I talk, taking in the multitude of ideas from our staff to improve our school for our students, staff, and families. Providing leadership opportunities for our staff has encouraged many of them to take on leadership roles whether they realize they are leading or not.

Our school has two main leadership opportunities: our grade-level teams and our building-leadership team. The great thing about our grade-level teams is that everyone on the team is a leader. Our grade-level teams consist of classroom teachers and a special education teacher. We meet weekly, and it seems there is a different leader or voice every week. Our meetings always start with kids, celebrating at least one student each week with a #GoodNewsCallOfTheDay as well as creating plans to support those students who are struggling a bit. We also talk about curriculum, schedules, and a variety of other topics. The agendas are open so that all staff on the grade-level team can add to the agenda. The best things about these meetings are the conversations we have and the relationships we build.

Our building-leadership team is amazing. We have one representative from each grade level, chosen by the grade-level teams, as well as one special education teacher, our school counselor, and our technology director. The team also has an open agenda, and we share shout-outs, concerns, and topics to discuss. This group is brutally honest with one another, and we all have the same status on the team. Our building-leadership team discusses professional development, schedules, workload and expectations, behavior expectations for our students, and many other topics. Every member of this team is a go-to person for me. They keep me grounded, and they have made our school better because of their focus on relationships with kids, staff, and families.

The job of principal is multi-faceted, and those you surround yourself with help to make you better. Empowering and engaging the staff you serve help to make the school a better place for everyone. Although there are times when a decision needs to be made by the principal without the input of others, those are few and far between. Involving individuals and teams in decisions, listening to their ideas, and reflecting on those decisions make our school an awesome place to learn.

—Jay Posick

AUGUST AND SEPTEMBER

As leaders, we have a responsibility to model positivity and enthusiasm. We can't expect our staff and students to be enthusiastic about things that we are not enthusiastic about. We do this by being excited about everything that school is about.

—Lead Like a PIRATE

Be relentless in seeking out and nurturing each person's greatness.

—Lead Like a PIRATE

When it comes to showing appreciation, August and September are some of the easiest months to make things happen. Think about it: You're all still in your honeymoon season, kids are still on their best behavior, and parents haven't gotten far enough along in the course of the year to have too many concerns. Education is one of the most incredible professions to be in because we get to do the "same" job year after year, but we get to have a refresh each summer or reset with each new school year. You're able to change up what you think didn't work from the year before. Perhaps you have staffing changes, or maybe you've changed positions or campuses; regardless, you have a chance to set the tone and energy for the upcoming year with however you welcome back your team. Typically, I (Amber) feel refreshed and as energetic as my team! New school clothes, new school supplies! Buildings are fresh and clean! Energy is high, and everyone is hopeful about the school year ahead. Why not reinforce all those positive vibes with some creative displays of appreciation that show your team members they have your full support? (Remember, you can actually use any of our ideas throughout the course of your school year!) Here are a few to get you started:

Welcome Back

When your teachers come back, set the scene with a little flair. If your school has a theme, it's a great time to tie in special decorations that will boost spirits. You can involve other teachers to help decorate or choose décor and activities.

Recognize Your Leaders

I (Amber) host a leadership day before all my teachers come back, and I work hard to make it a special time of retreat. We bond as a leadership team and discuss our plans and vision for the upcoming year. One year I surprised them with a special leadership T-shirt, a key chain, and a pack of colored pens. The key chains were super easy. I bought different "W" charms at Hobby Lobby and then looped them onto a key chain ring. They were only twenty-seven cents each! We went to lunch at a local restaurant and started our day together with some ice breakers but not the awkward get-out-of-your-seat kind. We did a this-or-that activity, and by disclosing fun preferences such as "jeans or skirts" and "tea or coffee," we learned more about one another's personalities and how they impact our teams.

This brings us back to where we discussed the different personality quizzes from earlier. Talking through my results or how I was typed, I let my staff know I wasn't given to sucking up, wasting money, or being disingenuous. It's literally how I'm made and think!

Sweet Treats

It's the start of a new year and a great time to spoil everyone around you just a little. We're not talking about an elaborate gesture, just a simple, sweet treat. Grab some popular snack cakes and make some fun, colorful signs.

- "Ding-dong, the bell's about to ring. Welcome back!" (Use Hostess Ding Dongs.)
- "Hi-ho, ho-ho, it's back to school we go!" (Use Hostess Ho Hos.)
- "Hope you're a happy camper about being back at school!" (Use Little Debbie Happy Camper Cakes.)
- "It's o-fish-ally time to get back to school!" (Use boxes of Pepperidge Farm Goldfish crackers.)
- "Here's hoping for a stress-free start to the school year!" (Use any stress-free antibacterial hand sanitizer, lotion, or soap.)
- "Here's to a year of all-new wishes; tonight you won't have to do the dishes!" (Use paper plates and forks.)

Along the way, keep an eye out for all those seasonal snack cakes. One year there were school bus brownies, and I think we bought out the store! We gave them to bus drivers and staff alike. You'll also want to add in some healthy options such as bottles of water, granola bars, or fruit. Some team members might want candy, while others might want to avoid carbs.

Walls of Appreciation

This has been a huge hit with my teachers and staff. Choose three different months out of the year and create a Wall of Appreciation! Write a personalized, handwritten note to each teacher and staff member and hang them on a decorated wall. After the month ends, place the notes in their mailboxes. You could also create a bulletin board where it becomes an appreciation station! String a clothesline across the board and add some clothespins. Then leave markers and note cards for people to air their "positive" laundry about each other!

Dessert Bar Social

Nothing fuels fun like dessert! This is an especially easy way for new teachers to connect with staff. Ask everyone to bring in their favorite dessert and then mix and mingle amid the yumminess!

Host a Breakfast

Invite your teachers and staff to a hot, delicious breakfast with you and your main office staff at the helm, flipping pancakes and scrambling eggs.

Friday Night Lights

We know a principal (Thanks, Sara Staley, for sharing!) who hosted a Friday-Night-Lights-style party as a back-to-school celebration. She issued all the teachers "tickets" to get in, and from the hours of 5:00 p.m. to 9:00 p.m., they enjoyed pizza, games, and lots of random prizes. She also handed out goodie bags that had been decorated to look like footballs, and inside were a variety of school supplies. (This is a pretty easy thing to have in your budget! You're going to stock up on pens, sticky notes, and markers anyway! Why not put them in pretty packages that make your teachers smile?)

Never Have I Ever

As a staff, complete a never-have-I-ever activity. This example was created and shared in our Principals Appreciation group, but it would be easy for an administrative or leadership team to create one as well.

Never have I ever Teachers Edition

When I was a student..never have I ever...

- cheated on a test
- made a prank phone call
- got in trouble for talking in class
- skipped school
- had braces
- gotten suspended
- shot spit balls
- had straight A's in school
- failed a class
- been the teacher's pet
- went to the bathroom to get out of doing work
- forged my parent's signature
- been called to the principal's office
- shared a sucker with my dog
- made up an excuse for missing homework
- toilet papered a house
- pretended to be sick to stay home from school
- performed in the talent show

When I was a teacher...never have I ever...

- taken a nap in my classroom
- accidentally said a bad word in front of my students
- left the copy machine jammed
- eaten food from the floor of my classroom
- fallen asleep in a meeting
- been called Mom or Dad by a student
- done something embarrassing in front of my students
- taken paper out of someone else's box when I ran out
- taken books from the library without telling the librarian
- broken the school rules
- pretended to be sick and stayed home from school

Prize Wheel

Another fun way to start the year is with a prize wheel. These spinners can be found on Amazon or at a teacher supply store. You simply change the prizes to fit what your campus enjoys or what your budget allows. The prizes don't have to be fancy! Jeans passes, leave-early passes, chocolate, and school supplies from the Dollar Tree are all great choices.

Backyard Cookout

One of my (Amber) new favorite traditions is a back-to-school cookout at my house. While my house is definitely not built to hold all seventy of our staff, the event works well as a laid-back, come-and-go gathering. We've done burgers, with my husband manning the grill, and we've done pizza, which was easy too! Teachers bring desserts or sides, and we just all hang out. It's really casual and has become a campus favorite!

Photo Booth

Create a back-to-school photo booth for your teachers. Stock it with campus swag, a fun background, and all kinds of props. You can find these in party stores or on Etsy, Teachers Pay Teachers, or Pinterest. Share them with your campus hashtag to get everyone excited about the new year! Invite your staff members' families to take pictures or receive swag too. We all know it takes a network of all our families for our teachers to give us their best. Acknowledging that our teachers have families who matter and are a part of your campus family go a long way!

Book Tasting

Depending on your budget, gifting your teachers with a professional development book can also be a way to tie professional development funds to a back-to-school celebration. I (Amber) have allowed our leadership team to host a book tasting for us at the beginning of each year. I give our leadership team a list of books in May that they can choose from. We buy the books, they read them over the summer, and then during PD, teachers have an opportunity to hear from their peers about why they should read certain books. Book tastings can be fancy with pretty table settings and centerpieces or casual with teachers floating from table to table. Our first year, before we had the leadership team read books, we asked authors to create a flip grid, "selling" their book to our staff. We had some incredible authors contribute videos explaining the passion behind their book, and staff were allowed to choose whichever they felt connected to. Teacher voice is important to me. I feel like if teachers have an opportunity to be connected in what we're trying to build, maybe they won't try to burn it down!

Here are a few books that we've read that have contributed to our culture:

- *The Innovator's Mindset: Empower Learning, Unleash Talent, and Lead a Culture of Creativity* by George Couros
- *The Wild Card: 7 Steps to an Educator's Creative Breakthrough* by Hope King and Wade King
- *Play Like a Pirate: Engage Students with Toys, Games, and Comics* by Quinn Rollins
- *50 Things You Can Do with Google Classroom* by Alice Keeler and Libbi Miller
- *The Zen Teacher: Creating Focus, Simplicity, and Tranquility in the Classroom* by Dan Tricarico
- *Unshakeable: 20 Ways to Enjoy Teaching Every Day . . . No Matter What* by Angela Watson
- *Be the One for Kids: You Have the Power to Change the Life of a Child* by Ryan Sheehy
- *Start. Right. Now.: Teach and Lead for Excellence* by Todd Whitaker, Jeffrey Zoul, and Jimmy Casas

- *Shattering the Perfect Teacher Myth: 6 Truths That Will Help You Thrive as an Educator* by Aaron Hogan
- *Ditch That Homework: Practical Strategies to Help Make Homework Obsolete* by Matt Miller and Alice Keeler

Postcard Station

Set the tone for a culture of encouragement by starting a postcard station during your professional development days. Provide each teacher with postcards for all their students. Give them the time to address all of them at one time, maybe at an in-service or staff meeting. We stamp each one with our mailing address so they are ready to be dropped into the mail after they are written. Your teachers are now able to jot quick, happy notes to their students throughout the year.

Escape Room

Create a teacher escape room to introduce all of your boring back-to-school content. We all know that you need to cover the basics, but why can't you make them a part of your theme and overall culture? You can do scavenger hunts, create videos with fun apps, or even have a tech rotation in which teachers introduce different creation tools to one another for back-to-school introductions.

Woot-Woot Wagon

I (Melinda) first heard of a "woot-woot" wagon from Stephanie McConnell, and the concept is simple: Instead of making your teachers come to the treats, take the treats to your teachers! The actual wagon itself can be a cart or anything on wheels. You can decorate it, add some portable tunes, or just keep it simple. Just be sure to fill it with all their favorite treats, and be prepared for all the smiles that will come your way!

Conclusion

When you think of starting the school year, you typically think of a fresh new start. This is an opportunity to start fresh with your team and allow the next chapter of your leaders to start the way that you want it to. If you think of each year like an airplane flight, one of the places where it can get rough is the take off. To ensure a smooth start, be intentional! With a little forethought and planning, adding just a couple of ideas will remind your team that you are conscious of how they are feeling and that recognizing their energy, hard work, and efforts matters to you. This allows them to feel energized to meet the needs of the students. It's a win-win for all!

Reflect on Starting Fresh

Leadership Treasure Hunt (Find This)

The beginning of the school year is a fresh slate! What is your personal goal and vision for the upcoming year?

Navigating the Seas (Think about This)

How can you communicate that goal and vision to your staff or team?

Charting the Course (Take Action)

Write down your goal and its meaning and share it with those around you. Sharing equals accountability and support!

Share your thoughts and ideas!
#LeadWithAppreciation

OCTOBER AND NOVEMBER: HONEYMOON IS OVER!

Every now and then the joker gets the better of us ... That's okay. We can assure you those times will pass.

—The Wild Card

Trade your expectation for appreciation and the world changes instantly.

—Tony Robbins

It's October. Fall is here. Pumpkin Spice lattes, flannels, and cute boots aside, this can be a challenging month for teachers. You are feeling completely overwhelmed. And so are your teachers.

You kicked the year off with a bang! Then what happened? New initiatives. Demands of district office. Meetings, meetings, and more meetings. Just like the teachers, all your good intentions go out the window with curriculum changes, new students, beginning-of-the-year sickness, and I could go on. (Insert your issues here.)

The honeymoon is over!

October is the first month where the new has worn off, but the hard work is still continuing. Typically you don't have a long holiday in October, and Thanksgiving break is still really far away. In the month of October, teachers have a chunk of instructional time and not a lot of "distractions" around to perk up the regular days. Most of the other months, except February, have a holiday to break up the course of the semester. I (Amber) have seen a dip in morale during these months. Those fall to-do lists can get intense!

In swoops the administrator to save the climate-and-culture day! October and November are very different months and should be handled in very different ways. Teachers need excessive amounts of support and grace during October, while November is a time to remember what you are thankful for and practice gratitude.

Remember, as the leader, we are *the person*. We have to be able to read our staff and intervene when necessary. We have to filter everything coming in so teachers can send out what our goal really is—producing learners and life-ready graduates. Teachers put more pressure on themselves than we'd like to think. Giving grace and acknowledging the climate in your building can go a long way!

Here are a few fun ways to show appreciation for your educators during the month of October:

Rubber Duckies

Fun and simple. Include a note that says, "Above the water, things roll right off, but I know you're paddling like crazy underneath. You got this!"

Boo Bucket

Start a "Boo!" bucket. This simple activity can be as easy as passing around a pumpkin bucket of candy with the instructions to pass it on to another coworker after you've had a treat. You can add a stack of the "You've been boo'd!" pages.

Teachers can hang the sign outside the classrooms to make sure they don't get the bucket back!

Parent-Teacher Events

On your parent-teacher conference night or another night during the season of conferences, provide dinner and ask parents to bring desserts.

Room Service

Place room service ordering forms on classroom doors to be turned in and filled the next day. This is so easy! Create a template with the treats you're offering, then leave the tag hanging outside the classroom door and pick up later in the day. Deliver the treats the next morning!

Kindness Bingo

Create a bingo board with different acts that staff and students can complete. Offer up an extra recess or jeans pass to those who complete a bingo. Teachers can only sign one box per day. Five in a row is a bingo! Activities can be geared towards campus or district initiatives.

Pudding Cups

Thank your staff for "Pudding" in the hard work! Hand out pudding cups and spoons to show them your support.

Orange Treats

Orange you glad it's October? Stock a table with all kinds of orange treats—mandarin oranges, orange pens, KitKats, Reese's, Cheetos, Doritos, fresh cantaloupe, sticky notes. Whatever you can find!

Raise the Bar

Praise your staff and faculty for raising the (candy) bar and hand out a variety of candy bar treats! I (Amber) like to just leave them in the front of their mailboxes.

Paydays

Who doesn't love payday? You can hand deliver pay stubs with a Payday candy bar each month. We also do #firstfriday treats in mailboxes. I (Melinda) print labels and stick them on for a quick tag. Pro tip: We use candywarehouse.com to bulk order most of our treats before school starts to take a little stress off during the school year. Print your labels and put them in gallon Ziploc bags labeled with the month before school starts. Done!

Conference Survival Bag

Create a fall conference goodie bag! The contents can change, but make sure to have water and go-to items like mints, caffeine, and easy snacks. Thanks to Michele Havighorst Stanton for this share!

November is the perfect month to focus on gratitude and everything we have to be thankful for personally and professionally. There is research about having gratitude and how it contributes to your happiness and quality of life. Shawn Achor, author of *The Happiness Advantage,* has the following on his website, bit.ly/leadWA3:

> *When we are positive, our brains become more engaged, creative, motivated, energetic, resilient, and productive. This discovery has been repeatedly supported by research in psychology and neuroscience, management studies, and the bottom lines of organizations around the world. Shawn Achor, who spent over a decade living, researching, and lecturing at Harvard University, draws on his own research—including one of the largest studies of happiness and potential at Harvard and at large companies like UBS and KPMG—to share strategies for how to fix this broken formula in* The Happiness Advantage. *Using case studies from his work with thousands of Fortune 500 executives in forty-two countries, Achor explains how we can reprogram our brains to become more positive, and ultimately, more successful at work.* This is something I have actually practiced for quite a few months.

We all go through things in life that can derail our level of gratitude and appreciation. The past few years have challenged me in ways I never imagined. I have lived a charmed life in comparison to others who have suffered unimaginable grief and violence. We also have to remember that our teachers are people too, and they are going through things we know nothing about. It's during the most trying times in our lives we count on others to lift us up. I am super blessed to have so many people near and far that helped me when I needed it the most. Administrators get to be—and must be—that supportive and uplifting person for their school community—even when it's hard.

Administrators get to be— and must be—that supportive and uplifting person for their school community— even when it's hard.

Gratitude Journal

For the past year, my gratitude journal has changed how I (Melinda) start my day. Every morning while making my coffee, I write down at least three things I am grateful for. This became a new habit by "anchoring it" to my existing habit of making coffee.

Fill the Fridge

Fill your fridge with snacks, drinks, and quick items your teachers can grab and go!

Apple Bar

Apple bar! (Our staff is BAR none! We made it to the end of the first core-ter!) Cut up apples and provide a bar of yummy toppings, including warmed caramel, chocolate syrup, melted marshmallow, nuts, yogurt, sprinkles, and more!

Thank-You Board

Create a "give thanks" bulletin board. Each teacher can have a bag, a card, or even just a sheet of colored paper. Add different "thanks" for everyone throughout the month. Each person can walk away with all kinds of appreciation from their peers.

Thirty Days of Gratitude

Observe, practice and celebrate thirty days of gratitude! Kristen Kuhlmann shared the chart below with her staff. What an engaging way to promote gratitude!

30 DAYS OF GRATITUDE - AHS STAFF

Tweet or post to our staff facebook page each day with a PHOTO!
Give a little explanation! Photos can be current or old!

Nov. 1	Who are you grateful for today?	Nov. 16	What movie are you grateful for?
Nov. 2	What item of clothing are you grateful for?	Nov. 17	What place on earth are you grateful for?
Nov. 3	What item in your home you are grateful for?	Nov. 18	What recipe are you grateful for?
Nov. 4	What activity you grateful for this weekend?	Nov. 19	What cozy place are you grateful for?
Nov. 5	What are you grateful for in your career?	Nov. 20	What tradition are you grateful for?
Nov. 6	What book are you grateful for having read?	Nov. 21	What are you grateful for on your day off?
Nov. 7	What are you grateful for during the month of November?	Nov. 22	What food item on your Thanksgiving table are you most grateful for?
Nov. 8	What kind of music or song are you grateful for?	Nov. 23	What are you grateful for on Black Friday?
Nov. 9	What pet/animal are you most grateful for in your life?	Nov. 24	What item do you use daily that you are grateful for?
Nov. 10	What hobby or sport are you most grateful for?	Nov. 25	What season are you grateful for?
Nov. 11	What physical activity are you grateful for?	Nov. 26	What ability/skill/talent do you have you are grateful for?
Nov. 12	What technology are you grateful for?	Nov. 27	What friendship are you grateful for?
Nov. 13	What appliance are you most grateful for?	Nov. 28	What store are you grateful for?
Nov. 14	What is something about your personality you are most grateful for?	Nov. 29	What is something outside you are grateful for?
Nov. 15	What place on earth you are grateful for?	Nov. 30	What moment this month are you most grateful for?

Daily Private Victory

Our staff leadership team took time out at the beginning of October to reflect on our year so far. One team member reminded us to find our daily private victory. Remembering your daily private victory keeps your passion alive. You will have to be intentional about this. It may not come natural to you to "celebrate" on a daily basis when that hasn't been your norm. I (Melinda) need visual reminders, and these reminders need to be posted right in front of my face, as in I almost need to literally trip over a visual reminder! When I can't remember a conversation in the hallway less than five minutes after I walk away, how will I remember to celebrate daily?

The daily private victory ribbon is posted right inside my door. I see it every time I walk out of my office. Most importantly, I see it when I walk out of my office at the end of the day. When you are inundated with paperwork, bus discipline, car duty in the rain, an unhappy parent, or an unhappy staff member, it helps to remember all the victories you have in your day.

Motivating and appreciating your staff are intentional practices that need to be built into your day. October is especially challenging for a variety of reasons. You can do this, and your staff can too.

Conclusion

When we are down and feel like we're about to be out, a simple word of appreciation or act of kindness can fill our bucket. It can be hard to see the goodness when we are swamped, buried, or stressed. But that is when we need gratitude and appreciation the most. That's why we want to be able to have something great for your staff to see when they go looking. Appreciation can make our best days brighter, and it is the one thing that can help us make it through the tough times. It is not frivolous. It is not a luxury. It is a coping strategy. And it works.

REFLECT ON OCTOBER AND NOVEMBER

 ## Leadership Treasure Hunt (Find This)

Kick start that gratitude journal by writing down at least three things you are thankful for today. They do not have to be huge things. Don't overthink it! Some examples are coffee, my kids, and the vet. (Maybe your dog was on death's door, and the vet worked miracles.) Do the same thing tomorrow, and the next day, and so on, and before you know it, your grati-tude journal is going strong!

 ## Navigating the Seas (Think about This)

What is your private victory today? Keep it simple. Example: I hit snooze only once.

 ## Charting the Course (Take Action)

Get it together! Plan four appreciation actions or gifts for your staff for the months of October and November. (Refer to our Principal Staff Appreciation & Motivation Facebook group for inspiration.)

Share your thoughts and ideas!
#LeadWithAppreciation

It's a Marathon, Not a Sprint

I love to run. I run for fun. I train, run races, run with a group, and run on my own. I often relate running to the job of an educator. Teaching students is much like running a marathon. Teachers cannot go out too fast and begin teaching without establishing relationships and a shared set of classroom expectations. On the contrary, they cannot start slow and sprint to the finish, as they may not be able to "get it all in" as they approach the finish line. The pace a teacher must find in building relationships, teaching, learning, and planning is just like hitting that pace-per-mile target.

Whether it's teaching or running, we go through spots where we get down on ourselves, feel alone, and begin to feel defeated. Just when we begin to feel we can't make it one more step or cannot possibly plan for one more thing, we turn the corner and there it is—the encouragement of a colleague, principal, or crazed fan just wanting you to keep putting one foot in front of the other.

I have been able to witness firsthand how a handwritten thank-you card brings a smile to a teacher's face, a teacher who was having one of those days. I have sat and listened to conversations during lunch, which I provided, leaving one less thing for a teacher to think about the night before or morning of. I have laughed with teachers over a scoop of ice cream when they decided to enjoy a little bit of sunshine and eat outside instead of working in their classrooms during lunch. Whether the encouragement comes in the form of food, words of affirmation, gifts, or a well-timed favor, the intentional time that leaders can set aside to show their appreciation for staff is critical.

—Matt Arend

DECEMBER

Predictable will never equal magical.

–The Wild Card

The biggest happiness is when at the end of the year you feel better than at the beginning.

–Henry David Thoreau

One of the most important ways you can connect with your staff is to know who they are and what they stand for. Knowing their story…their why…the things that matter to them, is at the very core of showing appreciation. We have mentioned several different ways that you can get to know them, but as we move into what can be a very traditional holiday season, make sure you've also done some getting to know them on this kind of personal level. We have many teachers with different faiths, values, and traditions that aren't as typically in your halls. Take into consideration any additional activities that can show your team that you value all that they bring into your campus space, not the ones you can easily find such as an activity on Pinterest. I've welcomed in mommas who want to share what they do at home with their students, and it has helped me further develop an empathy and appreciation for how very different our community and staff can be. It can be done through a survey or a conversation, but as the leader, set the tone that says you want to welcome and encourage all. *All* of these ideas in December can be adapted to meet the needs or traditions that your staff abides by; they don't all have to be traditionally centered. Be intentional about knowing and appreciating the diversity of your staff and then *use* that knowledge to plan some of your December activities.

December can be a month that might require some additional planning on your part, but it's also one that can leave your staff and families feeling supported, encouraged, and appreciated despite a season of stress. My secretary and I (Amber) typically think about what we want to "give" as our campus gift in early September so that we have enough time to get it ordered and put together. We use general funds for that gift, but this is a great opportunity to solicit help from your PTA or PTO or any community businesses that have offered to help support or encourage your team. If none have reached out, don't be afraid to reach out to them! The earlier you can do this, the better.

We also take part in a countdown to our winter break. We do a "Twelve days to . . . " but you can easily adapt that to the number of days you want to commit to doing small daily celebrations or treats. We send out a calendar in late November, so our staff has plenty of time to decide what days they are going to participate in and look forward to the most!

Here's an example of my (Amber) countdown to Christmas this year.

There are a variety of ways that you can share this with your team. I created mine in PowerPoint. I've also done it using Smore, an online newsletter template tool. Anyone can use the site to create event flyers, newsletters for students or parents, and other documents. Smore says its design tool is easy enough for first and second graders to use. Smore's educator version, available for a seventy-nine-dollar annual fee, automatically makes all flyers private. (I also use this site for our weekly staff emails and parent updates.)

Ideas for each day can be free, a small amount, or even just involve teamwork! This can be cheap and easy! Here is a list of ideas, just to get you started. Pick and choose or adapt to meet your campus needs!

- Snacks
- Hot chocolate bar
- PJ's, flannel, ugly sweater, fun clothes days! Pair with jeans and you can't go wrong!
- Soups for lunch (Have teachers sign up to bring their favorite or ask your parents to contribute!)
- Slushies or milk shakes (Drinks too much? Go buy Sonic ice, a variety of soft drinks, and have a soft drink spread for them to choose from. Just the ice makes it more fun!)
- Christmas song bingo (Play fun songs every hour on the announcements and give staff bingo cards! You can make them easily at myfreebingocards.com. You can also print out blank ones and have staff add their favorite songs to mix it up a bit!)
- Holiday photo booth
- Popcorn bar, with pre-popped popcorn and added toppings and throw-ins for an extra treat!
- Decorate Christmas cookies.

- Buy an assortment of cookies and have milk on hand! Pro tip: I bought almond and low-fat milk this year; it was a hit.
- Nacho bar
- Team build a gingerbread house and then have students vote.
- Have a Grinch-y salad bar with a variety of lettuce and fun toppings.
- Give the gift of time. Cover classes and let your teams enjoy an extra-long lunch!
- Host a PJ's and pancakes day. Have griddle, will travel! Ready-to-pour mix makes it easy to whip up a pancake extravaganza.

December can be a shorter month together, but you can still contribute to a positive climate with some of these activities!

- Find or make a giant cardboard form of Will from *Elf*, the movie, and let your staff take "elfies."
- Build a "Keep the Quote" spot in your hallways. Each week have someone find a fun quote to help motivate your team. The quotes can be seasonal or just plain fun and inspiring! (Kinders love fun anchor charts; let them take turns writing and decorating it!) Then each week, tear off the old and give it to a staff member to hang in in his or her classroom. Check out the #keepthequote on Instagram for great ways to stage the quote and ideas!
- Host a voluntary holiday dinner off campus. There can be a white elephant gift exchange for those who choose to come. Getting off site, even if your staff members are buying their own dinner, can be a way to bond and enjoy one another's company during a busy season.
- Have an ugly sweater competition amongst your staff.

- A fun twist on the ugly sweater idea—Have your teams design their own ugly sweater. Then have the students vote on which one is the "ugliest," and the principal has to wear it on the holiday party day!
- Create a holiday scavenger hunt of family traditions. Allow your teams to share at a staff meeting.
- Christmas gift bingo—There's a few things that you know are going to be popular gifts from your families (candles, cat coffee mugs, fuzzy socks). Create bingo boards and see who can win!

If you have members of your staff that celebrate Hanukkah, you can include them this month as well!

- Provide seasonal snacks, like fried pies or sugar cookies, or make sugar cookies into all kinds of fun Hanukkah shapes like Stars of David, dreidels, or menorahs.
- Provide menorahs for classrooms and have one in your front office.
- Pass around a blessing book. It can be just a simple journal that you pass around and allow each person to record the blessings that he or she has received throughout the year. The same book can be used in the following years.
- Have a latke cook-off amongst the staff! There are a variety of ways to make latkes, and this is a great way to have some healthy competition and a lot to eat.
- Fried cakes are a Hanukkah staple. Get some plain donuts, a lot of toppings, and have your staff decorate and fill their donuts as they please.

Part of appreciation is recognizing that all of our people are different. You may be a diverse staff and have the opportunity to celebrate a number of different holidays that may or may not be Christmas! All cultures celebrate appreciation; just be cognizant of the opportunity to make all feel included and celebrated . . . any of these ideas can be adapted to be as inclusive as possible, which of course, we advocate for!

Conclusion

This is an easy month for most to show appreciation or feel appreciated. It is no less important for you to be intentional, however! In what appears to be a month of excess, one of the simplest ways to show appreciation is that of time. Value your employees as human beings during the holiday season, with their own to-do lists and customs to celebrate.

Reflect on December

Leadership Treasure Hunt
(Find This)

Find a "give" for your team.
Will you make it or buy it?

Navigating the Seas
(Think about This)

Think about how you can share appreciation
with your families. What do they celebrate
in this season? How much do you share
about what matters to you?

Charting the Course
(Take Action)

Schedule a thoughtful holiday post to be shared
on social media when you are on winter break. It
can be an image, well wishes, or a thoughtful sen-
timent. Just an intentional connection with your
community and staff.

Share your thoughts and ideas!
#LeadWithAppreciation

JANUARY AND FEBRUARY

Cheers to a new year and another
chance to get it right.

–Oprah Winfrey

Happy New Year! In our profession, we are lucky enough to have two new years to celebrate—the start of each school year and the start of the calendar year. In this chapter, we are going to be talking about the new calendar year and returning to school in January after winter break. Winter break can be a whirlwind, but it can also be the respite and fresh start that many teachers need for the second half of the school year.

New Year's parties are not limited to adults. It's not rocket science that kids love parties. What if they came back from winter break to a red carpet, noise makers, and balloons? What a way to kick off the new year!

No one is better at New Year's celebrations for her school than the Pirate Principal herself, Beth Houf. She welcomes her kids and staff back with a party—complete with tacky prom or glitz-and-glam attire! She hands out noise blowers, throws glitter, and rolls out a red carpet, *à la* New Year's festivities. It was an eye-opening share! It never really dawned on me (Melinda) to celebrate the new year at school. I mean, it was over during break, right? What made it even more enticing is that all the New Year's decorations and props are on amazing sales right after January 1. You can buy them at a discount and make staff returning from their winter break that much more excited!

If you don't want to think about shopping for New Year's items, here's another activity with which you can kick off the month with your staff: They could choose their "one word" for the year. Instead of making and sharing resolutions, staff can choose just one word they can use as a focus for the upcoming year. There are many "craftivities" and ways to display one word. After the staff chooses their words, the kids can join in on the fun. You can create a one-word word cloud (check out wordclouds.com) and give it to teachers or hang it in your building. If you have a vinyl cutting machine, you can add those "one words" to a variety of products like clipboards, cups, mugs, and anything else that will sit still long enough!

- Make wishes for the new year (both personal and professional, shared and unshared) with the whole staff . . . then blow glitter in the wind like dandelion wishes! Thanks to the Facebook group Principal Principles for this great idea!
- Take around a hot cocoa cart on a particularly cold day. Stock up on cinnamon swirl sticks and fun marshmallows. Hand deliver to classrooms as a surprise.

Now it's on to February! Wait, what? It's February already? We just got back from winter break! In my (Melinda's) experience, February can bring some of the lowest morale of the year. (For those of you in the colder regions of the nation—indoor recess! Need I say more?) It's winter, and your school might or might not have a day off during February. The next break could be weeks away in March or April, which can seem so far away. You can make February fabulous! This is another month where the doldrums of long school days can set in. We hope that you can pick and choose from activities in this book, but this is another month where being intentional to lift spirits and encourage teachers will pay off in the long run!

I was introduced to Fabulous February more than fifteen years ago, but more recently, a fellow principal in my district, Dr. Rhonda Bishop, started perfecting her Fabulous February calendar. What was an idea in passing has evolved into a detailed activity that my staff looks forward to every year. She was a masterful planner when it came to special events for staff or students. At the time, Dr. Bishop was not yet on social media, and I began to share her ideas through my blog and eventually on Twitter and Facebook for other administrators to evolve and build upon. Now I can finally give her proper credit for the difference she made over the years. May Fabulous February live on forever!

Here are a few tips to help you get started:

Plan ahead.

This means before February 1. This isn't really a new concept for principals, so you're probably in good shape. Start planning early! Hopefully you included this when you sketched out your year before school started. Winter break is a great perfect time to plan. Create a "Fabulous February" list on your phone and add to it as you think of things. Word of caution: You will want to do everything. Ideas will pop up everywhere. FOMO (fear of missing out) is real at this point. You are human too. February is not necessarily your shining hour either. You will be giving a lot of yourself to parents, students, and teachers. Choose a few things to start with this year. It's easier to add activities in the future than to take activities away. You never know what activities are going to take off with your staff.

Recruit your secretary.

I could not pull off Fab Feb without my office staff. I have one full-time and one half-time secretary. They both help. We divide up tasks and start early in January. They love it! Okay, let me clarify. They enjoy being able to do fun things and bring joy. Some of the tasks leading up to the event might not be their favorite way to spend time.

Another principal in my district, Kara Crighton-Smith, created a theme calendar for her February. Why didn't I think of that? Below are some theme ideas that I (Melinda) have tried.

- Fun Fridays: Fridays are a great place to start celebrating in February. Choose four to five activities for your staff to enjoy on Fridays. This gives you the whole week to plan and delegate. You can break your activity up into daily tasks for you and your secretary so it's not one huge project for either one of you.

- Fabulous Foods of February: This is another way to streamline activities. Maybe all your events revolve around food. Small snacks and drinks are easy to come by. Does your school have a popcorn machine? Is a local restaurant or business able to donate something? Parents love to help! Post an online sign-up for desserts or treats and parents could provide the work and food.

- Fashionista February: Different outfits of the day. Jeans Day, Polka Dot Day, Work Out Wednesdays, Gaudy Jewelry Gala, etc. The nice thing about dress-up days is that you can involve the students, and they will love it. It's not a lot of work for anyone.

- Souper Bowl: Elicit help from parents to bring a "soup-er" lunch for your staff.

- Chocolate Fountain: Fresh fruit, melted chocolate—what's not to love?

- Secret Pal: This is the same concept as a secret Santa but centered around Valentine's Day. Parameters can be established as you see fit for your people: duration, price limit, etc.

- Cupid Cart: Wheel around your fun cart full of favorite treats and drinks. Let teachers choose something they "love."

- You're the balm!: Let your staff know they are the "balm." Amazon sells bulk Chapsticks that you can hand out to your teachers. This is a favorite for both your female and male staff!
- You have a pizza my heart: Serve your staff pizza for lunch!
- We all *scream* for Fridays!: Help yourself to an ice cream treat in the lounge freezer!
- You are *all that* and a bag of chips: Attach a fun note to lunch-sized chip selections and let them choose their favorite!
- Chili cook off: Have staff bring in their favorites and have a chili tasting contest. Invite your superintendent over to be the judge!

- Give out Bitmoji bookmarks: Add your Bitmoji to a bookmark (Template found on Amber's blog—just search "Bitmoji!")

- Couples challenge: This one is always a hit! Find pictures of popular celebrity couples. Cut them in half and leave one half on each teacher's desk. The challenge is to find their match, without using technology! You can mix this up with old and new favorites, from famous tv couples (Fred and Ethel) to new matchings (Justin and Haley). One year I stalked Facebook and found couple pictures of our staff and used those! I gave baked treats (banana bread) for the first five couples to find their match.

- A Flair-ly easy treat: Give your teachers Flair pens (either a couple each or a whole pack!) and tell them how Flair-y awesome they are!
- Share the love! Cut out paper hearts and have available for staff to write each other heart-happy notes. You can ask students and parents to contribute as well. Hang them around the building or stuff mailboxes!
- Fizzy Drink Friday: Have a varied assortment of drinks or make a gas station or Sonic run to fuel up your team!
- Cookies and milk: Who doesn't love Oreos and milk? Have an assortment of cookies and milks for staff on your woohoo wagon or treat cart for them to choose from. I've added 2-percent milk, whole milk, and even almond milk to make sure I've covered all my bases!
- Share the "encourageMINT!": Add positive happy quotes on labels to the little boxes or rolls of mints and encourage staff to tweet out different encouragements for others! (Find the tic tac template on Amber's blog, amberteamann.com)

If February gets away from you, don't fret because there is always Marvelous March and Awesome April! (Or turn these ideas into Jubilant January!)

Conclusion

This is another month during which morale can drop. December is a fond memory, and Spring Break seems far away. No matter what the cause, low morale requires a pro-active response from you as a leader. While you might not be able to change what's going on in the broader sense of the school year, you can foster an environment that's more productive and rewarding for your team. Many of these ideas will have your staff looking forward to February rather than it being a slump of a month!

Reflect on January and February

Leadership Treasure Hunt
(Find This)

Visit *The Principal Blog* or *Technically yours, Teamann* for more examples of Fab February.

Navigating the Seas
(Think about This)

What is manageable for you and your staff in February?

Charting the Course
(Take Action)

Create. Delegate. Implement. Enjoy!

Share your thoughts and ideas!
#LeadWithAppreciation

Gratitude in Ten Minutes or Less

We all like to think we're grateful, but gratitude requires action, and too often it simply falls through the cracks. The day-to-day demands of leading a school can become routine for any administrator. Answering emails, attending meetings, greeting students, supervising the lunchroom—the list of everything we must to do to keep our schools running successfully is endless! But what if there were a way in ten minutes or less each day that you could also share gratitude with those around you?

I started hanging out in the hallways of my middle school to get more connected with the students. In the mornings, I check out multiple hangouts to connect with students, check in with a few, and make sure that I am modeling the transparent and visible leader I work to be every day. The added benefits to this daily interaction are the informal and intentional connections I make with staff. I know that down one hall, I can check in with the eighth-grade math teacher to see how the recent Math Olympiad competition went. If I head down to the gym area, I can see the PE teachers playing a game of ball with a group of students, and even in the cafeteria, I can check in with teachers who are helping make sure breakfast runs smoothly and is a positive start to the day. After those interactions, I always find one specific, small thing to thank the staff member for doing. It could be an interaction I saw them have with a student, the volunteer efforts they gave at a recent dance, or just a lesson I observed from the hallway. A school leader's words matter, so make sure they're intentional, frequent, and full of praise.

We have all sent a positive note home with a student at one time. I actually still have a few powerful notes I received as a student myself. But what about sending gratitude and celebration notes home with staff members? Each year I find a new way to send home a note in the mail to staff. One year it surrounded specific praise of implementation of an initiative, and the next year I wrote them as I did my regular walkthroughs. One year I changed it up and sent it to a family member of the staff member! When engaging in this type of endeavor, remember that all means all. Include everyone on your school team—paraprofessionals, office workers, custodians, cafeteria workers, part-time staff, and regular substitute teachers! The impact of this gesture is well worth the work involved. Too often we go through the day-to-day and don't stop to celebrate the little things that make our school great. Find a few minutes, grab some special notecards, and start writing about the amazing things that happen each day because of every staff member committed to the vision for your school.

I saw this one on the internet, and at first, I was hesitant. I mean, a "treat trolley" at a middle school? During my first year? I was sure they would think I was nuts, but I was wrong. They loved it! In December a volunteer and I went around the school and offered teachers treats from the cart as a special thank you for the work they do. We made sure to catch all staff and had a set of treats in the lounge as well. Due to the success of that one opportunity, I have brought in snacks for special holidays and after the tenth snow day of the third quarter. (No joke—ten!)

While I can't always change the conditions we are given, I can celebrate the staff for everything they do to overcome the circumstances to create success for our kids. And there is a little fun in finding creative ways to say thank you for such a job well done.

—Jessica Cabeen

MARCH AND APRIL

Can't keep calm. It's March Madness.

—somewhere on the Internet and in every classroom

Spring is nature's way of
saying, "LET'S PARTY!"

—Robin Williams

Springtime can be beautiful and energizing, but the season can also feel a little long—regardless of where your Spring Break falls on the calendar. Showing appreciation in creative ways helps interrupt some of that monotony and gives teachers just the boost they need to keep going. As with any season, it's fun to pair your gestures with current holidays, but you can incorporate most any of our ideas at any time during the school year. You can also recycle certain ideas to suit your needs.

Here are some of our favorite ways to show appreciation during the spring:

Fill a Basket

The Easter holiday—which might fall in March or April depending on the year—looms large during the spring, so it helps to keep an eye out for inexpensive Easter basket stuffers to use as motivators, encouragers, or just regular day brighteners. I (Amber) again default to Little Debbie treats, as they have seasonal favorites that are easy to use. For my office staff, a team of six, I can leave a treat on their desks, thanking them for all they do, for less than three dollars. Baskets of treats are also an easy way to honor and recognize a large group of people without breaking the bank. If your building is running smoothly each day as an efficient machine, it's not just you making that happen. As a school administrator, you know it takes your entire team—everyone from teachers and secretaries to janitors and nurses—so make sure they all feel seen and valued and appreciated.

Mardi Gras

No self-respecting New Orleanian would be caught eating king cake, wearing beads, or listening to "Mardi Gras Mambo" after Fat Tuesday, so plan accordingly! You can usually find all of these fun props in most grocery and discount stores—and don't forget to stock up on purple, green, and yellow paper! One fun activity is to create an "acts of kindness" board. For every act your team members complete, they get beads to wear or hang in their offices or classrooms. (You can include students as well. Beads are cheap and acts of kindness never go out of style!) Contact a local bakery or grocery store to see if it would be willing to donate a king cake for your staff. If you can't find one to be donated, you can take an easy shortcut with a Bundt pan and several cans of cinnamon rolls! Melt the icing to top it off and sprinkle with purple, green, and yellow sprinkles. Leave an iPad or another streaming music device in your lounge, setting the scene with tunes such as the Dixie Cups' "Iko Iko" and Al "Carnival Time" Johnson's "Carnival Time."

March Madness

If Mardi Gras isn't your thing, think sports and a March Madness bracket! There are so many variations on the traditional college basketball bracket. (These days, brackets are especially easy to create online!) Hang a large, colorful bracket in your lounge or office area and work your way through any number of quirky contests until you have a champion. Quick and easy games like shuffleboard, ping pong, or Connect Four work well, and a big favorite is an Oreo Challenge. Have all the different flavors of Oreos for staff to taste test and vote on until there is an ultimate winner. This is also fun because National Oreo Day is celebrated March 6. In the same vein, Pi Day is March 14. Invite your team to bring in their favorite pie recipes for a Pieapalooza! They bring the pies, and you supply the plates and forks! Another fun option is to create a Best Picture Book Bracket, bringing in guest readers, holding read alouds, and having students vote on their favorite books.

My Bracket

One campus went all out for their brackets and had an entire month of competitive fun! Valery Fuhrman shared the following ideas and used the bit.ly/leadWA4 to create the bracket. All staff was initially included. If members chose not to play, they had to let her know, and their match automatically advanced by a forfeit. Winners notified the office, and that's how the bracket advanced.

- Round One: Rock, Paper, Scissors Challenge; Players let the office know who wins to move forward.
- Round Two: Dice Dash; Players roll one die ten times and add the total of their rolls. The player with the highest total advances to the next round. (Dice are made available in the office if needed!)
- Round Three: WAR! Divide a deck of cards evenly and play one round of the card game WAR. Play through the stack once, and the player with the most cards after the first round advances. (Decks of cards are made available in the office if needed!)
- Round Four: Jenga! Play during a staff meeting, and the player who knocks over the tower first is eliminated.
- Round Five: Connect Four; The player who gets the first connected four advances! (Games are available in the office!)
- Round Six: Checkers! This round can be completed during a staff meeting.

Winner of the overall games can be gifted an early release one Friday afternoon.

How fun would this be if you had a competitive staff? Bracket contests would definitely keep everyone on their toes throughout the whole month!

Additional ideas for the month of March are:

- Allow staff and students to wear their favorite alma mater or college T-shirts.
- Share pre-written "apology" notes just in case you get the "spring blues." (These would be *hilarious* to write and have available!)
- Have a student-versus-teacher shootout competition—kickball, running, cartwheels, somersaults, or some other fun activity.
- Allow staff and students to wear warm ups.
- Have a Chip and Dip Day.
- Allow staff and students to wear crazy socks.
- Treat campus to ice cream sundaes.
- Have sticky notes and Sharpies near the staff mailbox for everyone to share some love with a quick note to one another!
- Have everyone bring in a bag of their favorite candy and share the bounty to get through the week.
- Allow teachers to have their favorite—permitted—drinks in the lounge.
- Treat teachers with a coffee bar with toppings, syrups, and yummy creamers available.

By the time April rolls around, you might be looking for even more activities to carry you through the rest of the year. Remember that any of the ides in this book can be used at any time of the year, so don't let yourself be limited by the month or title. Switch it around, mix it up—whatever you need to do to make it work for you and your people!

The following ideas are just a hodgepodge that can be rolled out in April or any other time:

- April Fools' Day! Tape a small image to the bottom of each teacher's mouse, covering the optical lens. Panic will ensue!
- Take a "treat trolley" around and let each staff member pick an egg that could have anything from a piece of candy to a $25 Amazon gift card! (If you can't use Amazon, choose a vendor that fits your needs. Gift cards can be donated by parents, and the Amazon instructional gift card can be purchased through your school account.)
- "What Do You Meme" Teacher activity! It's like Apples to Apples or Cards Against Humanity. Each person takes five phrase cards, one person draws a meme card, and the rest choose which phrase from their hand would go with the meme. The player who chooses the meme selects the best match. (If you don't have time to create your own, find a template in our Facebook group!)
- If your staff can handle bathroom humor, hand out "Our teachers are stinking awesome" cookies, cupcakes, or brownies with poop emojis.
- Learning is in Full Bloom! Place random kinds of candy in little flower pots.
- Throw a confetti egg party. (This idea comes from Jennifer Vest.) Buy or make confetti eggs, making one a special glitter egg. Have each participant choose two eggs. Smash the eggs on one another's heads but no throwing and no poking eyes! The lucky winner who gets the glitter egg smashed on his or her head gets the special prize—a chocolate bunny rabbit to take home.
- Old-school egg hunt. Schedule a staff meeting and announce there will be an egg hunt. Hide eggs inside or outside your building. I (Amber) have filled ours with everything from

candy to numbers, and they have to come back in and choose their prize. Stationery, candy bars, and even bean bag chairs have been some of the prizes I have offered! (My team used book fair points to purchase larger items!)

- Peeps for your peeps. Wrap up peeps with a fun message attached, such as "Peeps for our peeps!"

- One-two-three-four, I declare a Peeps war! Campuses can level up their egg hunts by having a hidden peep war. If having candy all over your building stresses you out, opt for eggs!

- Give Reese's peanut butter eggs and attach a note that says, "We think you're an EGG-cellent teacher!"

- Give out "rainbow seeds" (bags of Skittles) and attach a fun rhyme, such as "A rainbow ahead, blue skies above, thanks for all you do, 'plant' these seeds with love!"

- Egg a coworker. Set up a plastic-egg filling station. Have slips for happy notes and a bucket of plastic eggs for teachers to fill out and stuff for their coworkers. Add some pieces of chocolate or little prizes then prepare the notes or let them write their own.

- Take a chance, choose a challenge. This activity centers around acts of kindness. Take a red Solo cup and put in an "act of kindness." (Pinterest can provide a ton of ideas.) Using a rubber band, cover the top of the Solo cup with foil and hang on a bulletin board or set out on a table. Choose a quote to accompany the display, such as "If we all do one random act of kindness daily, we might just set the world in the right direction," and let teachers choose!

- Thank everyone for chipping in. Have an assortment of chips and dips for staff to choose from to show your team you've noticed their teamwork.

- Have a regift party. Ask your staff to donate any "extra" gifts they have lying around. Think lotions, candles, mugs, and so on. You'll want as many gifts as you have staff members. I (Amber) supplemented with budget-friendly items like Chapsticks, car deodorizers, and nail files. My team numbered each prize, put the numbers in plastic eggs, then hid them all around the school. As teachers found the eggs, they came to the office to claim their prizes.

Conclusion

March can be madcap, and April can be full of showers, but you will survive. With these ideas, you can even invite the sunshine of spring inside your walls. Busy days are sure to turn into busy weeks, which turn into busy months and years, but we must always remember to stop and celebrate all our successes. Taking the time to recognize your team members for a job well done in their day-to-day work is never a waste, and it's one of the easiest, cheapest, and most effective ways to boost morale.

Reflect on Springtime!

Leadership Treasure Hunt
(Find This)

Choose two activities to integrate into your campus plans for March and April. Make a list of needs that your secretary can watch for.

Navigating the Seas
(Think about This)

Are you meeting a variety of the needs for your campus?

Charting the Course
(Take Action)

Have you extended your appreciation to someone outside your campus? Take a minute to write a note of thanks to someone now!

Share your thoughts and ideas!
#LeadWithAppreciation

TEACHER APPRECIATION

Say "Thank you!" Thanking people for the
work they do is important, and we simply
can't do it often enough!

–Lead Like a PIRATE

Appreciation can make a day, even
change a life. Your willingness to put
it into words is all that is necessary.

–Margaret Cousins

Cue Barry Manilow–looks like we made it! Finally, it's May. Sunshine. Maybe some flowers by now. Spring is here, and most of all, it's Teacher Appreciation Week. We saved the best for last. This is the Super Bowl and Daytona 500 of our appreciation efforts! This is when we take it up a notch.

A good thing to remember about this week is it's not about you. It's about the teachers. Please don't set yourself up for disappointment by expecting appreciation or thanks in return for appreciation. Your teachers will appreciate it, and they will be thankful. That goes without saying—especially if you have been showing your appreciation in small ways throughout the school year. This week, however, is special. This week is the finale!

If you plan like me (Melinda), you have a few things in place. If you plan like Amber, you are ready. Whatever your tendency, whether you have been planning for months, or you're in a last-minute rush, we've got you. We want to give you everything you need to make this week a tremendous success. Just a word of warning—don't try to do everything we suggest all in one Teacher Appreciation Week. And don't forget to delegate. The more hands you have helping, the better the week will feel for you and everyone involved.

Here we will share some of our favorite ideas and tips for making your Teacher Appreciation Week the best one yet.

Choose Your Theme

A theme can make this week much easier to plan because it can narrow your choices when it comes to food, decoration, gifts, and much more. Here are a few to consider:

Best Teachers in the World

Decorate with paper airplanes, suitcases, maps, and globes. Each day feature a different country and its unique customs and treats. Think English tea and coffee cake or a Mexican nacho bar. Welcome your teachers to Sweden with spa day. Transform an available room with soft music, essential oils, flavored water, lotions and maybe a massage chair! (Thanks to Andrea Keller for sharing these great ideas!)

Camp _____ (Your school name here!)

Invite your team out into the great outdoors with a fun camping theme. Decorate with tents, backpacks, picnic tables and baskets, and red and white checked picnic blankets. Be prepared and hand out teacher survival kits with everything from lip balm and hand lotion to gums and mints. Each day can feature a different trail mix, and you can treat teachers with all kinds of camping food, such as hotdogs and individual s'mores.

Candy Land

Inspired by the classic Hasbro board game, this week is all about sweets for the sweet! Transform different rooms in your building into fanciful spaces, such as Cookie Commons, Gummy Hills, Chocolate Mountain, and Peppermint Pass. The possibilities are endless—and delicious!

Time Machine

Celebrate through the decades with decorations, costumes, and snacks. For the 1950s, don your poodle skirts and roller skates and serve up milkshakes. Have an elegant 1960s *Breakfast at Tiffany's* breakfast bar. For the 1970s, wear tie-dye and bell bottoms and hand out colorful flower bouquets or give your team a Sesame Street and Cookie Monster milk-and-cookies treat. Throw a 1980s *Urban Cowboy* barbeque or a 1990s *Fresh Prince of Bel Air* dance off! Keep in mind that Amazon sells all kinds of candy from different decades, and don't forget the music to fully set the scene. (Thanks to Lissa Archuletta for these great ideas!)

Bon Voyage!

Send your teachers on a much-deserved ocean cruise! Each day can be a different port of call with unique decorations and food.

Incorporate games—shuffleboard and hula hoops in the hallway—or pamper teachers with mini-pool foot spas and lounge chairs!

Life's a Beach

Turn your building into a relaxing tropical paradise. Decorate with real sand, blue water, beach towels, beach balls, floaties, toy sharks, and colorful beach umbrellas. Food ideas include popsicles, snow cones, umbrella drinks, and maybe a seafood lunch!

A Royal Celebration

Celebrate with a princess and prince theme; wear your favorite ascot or fascinator. Treat your team to tea and crumpets one afternoon. Bonus points if they are served with a British accent!

All A'buzz about Your Staff!

Plan a yellow-filled week with a honeybee as your central character. Snacks, gifts, décor, all sunshiny and bright!

Take an Uber!

Let your teachers call an "Uber" (you and your office staff or central office personnel) during their planning period to ferry them to a nearby gas station or fast-food restaurant for a pick-me-up snack or drink!

Walk the Red Carpet

Decorate with a literal red carpet and meet your teachers at the door with feather boas, bow ties, and tiaras! Make up swag bags filled with everything from hand sanitizer to Sharpies and serve up ginger ale in fancy cocktail glasses. You can hand out awards to teachers throughout the week, emphasizing their amazing talents and gifts.

When it comes to themes, our best advice is to simply choose one and run with it. Google everything you can about your theme, start a working list, and brain dump everything digitally or on paper. Share it with everyone on your planning team—with the intention of narrowing down later on—and you're sure to get the ideas flowing!

Plan the Food

It's actually helpful to start with a few questions. What's your budget? How many people will you need to feed? Will you provide food and drinks every day? Who will pick it up and deliver it to classrooms? How much help do you have to make all of this happen? Remember that it will be May, and you will be just as busy as the teachers—if not busier—so the more hands, the better. At this time, it's also a good idea to revisit your teachers' favorite things and diet-and-allergy restrictions.

Here are some more of our favorite food ideas:

Happy Hour

Serve up a variety of fun and frozen non-alcoholic mocktails in the teacher's lounge complete with pretzels, peanuts, wings, and mini tacos!

Fancy Coffee Bar

Brew hot and iced coffees with a variety of toppings and syrups.

Thank-You Drinks

Individual or custom-made drinks delivered to classrooms with a note that says, "Thanks for quenching our thirst for learning." At the beginning of each school year, many dollar stores put cute water bottles on sale. You can add labels to the bottles featuring names, hashtags, or your school name and fill them with candies and random goodies.

Galaxy Far, Far Away

You can have Princess Lays, Yoda Soda, Vader-ade, and chocolate Darth Vader cookies that will lure everyone to the dark side!

Chocolate Fountain

Set up a fondue oasis where teachers can dunk everything from cookies to fruit in white, dark, and milk chocolate for a midday snack.

One Big Meal

This kind of celebration would need a great deal of advance planning. Catering can be expensive, but parent-teacher organizations can help out tremendously. Depending on your school district's policies, you might be able to secure donations from local businesses or churches.

Communicate

Communicate, communicate, communicate! Rally the troops early. Start advertising at least a month ahead of your celebrations. Be prepared to send lots of reminders. Life is busy. It's busy for you, your teachers, the parents, everyone. Reminders are helpful. I (Melinda) can't remember a parent or staff member who got upset over too many reminders. Send reminders at least weekly to keep the ball rolling. My teachers get a copy of the plan for the week on cute paper like Astrobrights. There are usually a lot of moving parts during this week. We have kids, parents, district office personnel, and community members

playing a role. If kids are going to bring gifts or supplies, I like the teachers to have a heads-up. (You never know what kids might bring to school as "gifts" for their teachers.) Everyone has good intentions when it comes to appreciating teachers. Good intentions are not always followed by actions. Reminders are sent with good intentions.

Social Media

Whether it's Facebook, Twitter, Instagram or another platform, get ready to explode your feed with celebrations, reminders, and even live events. If you start the week with a social media plan, the rest of the week should fall into place. Be loud when you're being proud! Here's a sample five-day plan:

Kid Videos

- Use the app Quik to ask ten kids what makes a great teacher.
- Parent Videos
- During drop-off and pick-up times, ask parents to give a shout to your staff that you can share with your team.
- Highlight each grade level or department throughout the week. Share out a brag or shout out via your social media channels until you've celebrated each staff member. I (Amber) create a template so that all I have to do is drop in a pic of the teacher in action and a sentence or two about how great he or she is!
- Make and share thank-you videos. Record teachers thanking everyone for a fabulous week.

Alert the powder monkey: If you don't know what a powder monkey is, you *must* get *Lead Like a PIRATE*! It's a concept discussed in the book by Shelly Burgess and Beth Houf of someone who is pressed into service! In this case, my secretary is the powder monkey. Life happens. The unexpected happens. Someone needs to know the plan for the week as well as you do. Whether it's your secretary, assistant, school counselor, or PTO president, make sure someone could pull the week off if you were not there. I know that's a little dramatic, but you just never know.

Conclusion

While every campus has a different budget, crew, and tradition when it comes to teacher appreciation, this is a week where, as the leader, you can let some of the simplest words of appreciation showcase the thankfulness you feel. A cute or fun format matters less than being genuine. Amplify your show of appreciation of those around you. Let your teachers feel the overall message of gratitude for their contributions to what matters most: their time, energy, and dedication to what they do. Throw in some glitter and everyone wins!

A cute or fun format matters less than being genuine.

REFLECT ON TEACHER APPRECIATION

Leadership Treasure Hunt
(Find This)

Share through all of your communication
channels that Teacher Appreciation
Week is here.

Navigating the Seas
(Think about This)

How can you communicate to
your team your appreciation?

Charting the Course
(Take Action)

Consider publicly thanking your
team members for what they do.

Share your thoughts and ideas!
#LeadWithAppreciation

Reach Out to Those around You!

Showing staff members how much we appreciate them for their hard work and dedication to our students is extremely important to enhance the positive culture within the school. Leaving notes, small tokens of appreciation, door prizes, and hosting teacher appreciation events can all add up. Most school districts have a very small budget to fund these gems. Here is what has worked for me: Know your community, your parents, and your rock star secretary! As a principal, I can often come up with some great ideas, but the problem comes in the form of time and money. Parents and local businesses help out a great deal. I allow them to advertise on the Sonic drinks they provide or let them put a pamphlet in the teacher's boxes. My secretary is amazing at making phone calls for donations, enlisting volunteers, and assembling some of our little gems for the staff. Principals can get caught up in other business, and it is nice to have someone who can follow through with your plan when you are pulled away.

Homecoming in our small Texas town is a big deal, from prekindergarten through twelfth grade. As an elementary campus, we like to have a little fun ourselves. We have had our very own homecoming court. My assistant principal and I made sashes to wear and were pulled around on a dolly up and down the hallways, waving and throwing candy to the students while wearing 1980s prom attire. (My assistant rocked a short, brightly colored, sequin number!) The teachers got a great laugh, and guess who pulled the dolly? That amazing secretary I mentioned earlier. We also threw out tokens for the teachers, and they were able to redeem their tokens later for a prize. Another year we rolled into every classroom and had a brief homecoming dance. This allowed the students a quick break with some fun and entertainment. Teachers were given a snack as we danced! Who can forget the homecoming float? We had our own float with root beer and coke floats for the teachers! They made sure to be present when our float passed through the hallway.

Teacher Appreciation is a week that I consider my "pirate week." I love to make this a fun week for everyone and see how excited they are to come to school each day. Our week consists of a week-long theme. Themes I have done include Candyland, Baseball, and Pac-Man. There is a competitive video shown each morning that we have prerecorded. Teachers pick a winner each morning, and the whole class watches in anticipation. Will Pac-Man level up or be eaten by a ghost? Winners receive a prize! This is where donations and business sponsors come in handy. It is fun to see on the videos, "Today's game was brought to you by___." The whole class is excited if their teacher wins! We also have little tokens throughout the day that go along with the theme and lots of food! Being dressed up during the day as a character, decorating your common areas and lounge around your theme, and those words and tokens of affirmation help to bring your teacher appreciation to the next level. I'm currently working on "cooking" up the next teacher appreciation.

Just remember—you do not have to do this alone. Reach out to those around you!

—Sara Staley

Self-Care for Administrators

Leading like a PIRATE can be exhausting.
Taking time to rest is imperative to truly
be your best you!

—Lead Like a PIRATE

We believe that self-care is not selfish,
and in fact, being healthy allows
us to be more selfless.

—Balance Like a Pirate

Now it's your turn. That's right, you. You can't fill other people's buckets when your bucket is empty. As a leader, it's critical to remember that you must take care of yourself.

When you arrive at work or school every morning, there's no airplane flyover or fancy welcome. You're barely inside the door

You can't fill other people's buckets when your bucket is empty.

before being hit with a barrage of questions to answer, problems to solve, and phone calls to return. For many school administrators, the only thing that remains the same about their jobs is that nothing stays the same. When your brain is constantly bouncing, solving, and assisting, it makes sense that at any given moment, you might be exhausted and running low on positivity. On a daily basis, leaders generally get little positive feedback. When was the last time someone wrote you a happy gram, brought you coffee in the morning, or verbally thanked you for your hard work and late nights? We bet it's been a while, and that can be disheartening. While you don't work for accolades or expect to receive them every day, it feels good to be appreciated. The harsh truth, however, is that we cannot wait for others to take care of us. We must take care of ourselves and show ourselves the appreciation and love we need to keep going.

One way to practice self-care is to achieve more balance. Balance as a leader is difficult. Gauging how much of your energy you're dedicating to all the different hats you wear can be daunting. Whether you're mom to one or none, married or single . . . there are people other than your staff who want the very best version of you that they can get.

Have you ever kept track of the positive vs. negative inputs in your day? Try it just one day. Within an hour I bet you'll have lost track and are just going through your day as usual. Because we have *so* many interactions, it's easy to lose track of how quickly we can lose our bounce. According to researchers Sahakian and Labuzetta, various internet sources estimate that an adult makes about thirty-five thousand remotely conscious decisions each day. Is it any wonder that you're tired and depleted? It's easy to see how the self-care aspect of who we are as leaders can fall to the wayside. We wanted to ensure that in addition to knowing that we need to take care of our people, we also need to take care of ourselves.

Outside of leadership, we are human too. Our teachers are human, and our students are human. There are people who have been through so much worse than what I have experienced. There are social justice issues that are very relevant in our nation right now, and we can't assume that a gift or a snack is going to turn around the mindset that we or some of our staff are in. If we don't take care of ourselves while we are throwing ourselves into a strong and positive leadership, we won't make it.

After going through some significantly difficult life experiences, I (Melinda) had to get my head right. My own negative self-talk was weighing me down and not helping me or anyone in my orbit. I figured out that a great way to gauge that negative self-talk is to imagine yourself saying all those same things to a trusted colleague or friend. It's horrifying! Chances are most of us would never dream of doing such a thing, so why do it to ourselves?

I (Melinda) have lived a somewhat charmed life. My parents were married for fifty years. I had two awesome brothers. Got every job I wanted. I have been in the same district for twenty-five years at the time of this book. Married with two amazing daughters. I own my home, and the only college debt I have is from graduate degrees that are almost paid off.

Remember when I just said that I lived a charmed life? Well, my daughters haven't. In the span of just a few short years, their uncle died, their dad left, their dog died, and their Papa passed away tragically. It was a dark time in all our lives . . . and this is the reality of all our worlds. I have heard that your "mess is your message." We are supposed to be the leader of the message, and the "upkeeper" of culture, but it can be hard when our personal lives are in a dark place.

One helpful self-care strategy is for educators to remind themselves of why they started in the field in the first place. Most of us became educators to make a difference. I imagine you became a leader because you wanted to increase your influence. My girls are who I live my life for every day. They are my why and the reason I work so hard to have a positive mindset.

What is your why? Do you remember?

I love working with kids.

I want to make a difference in the world.

It's a calling, not a job.

In the beginning, there was a fundamental reason that you loved your job. Whether it's teaching to a small group or standing out front each morning and greeting your students with big hugs, there is a happy place for you in your position. Get out of your office and go see the incredible things that are happening in your building. Sometimes I take a laptop and go work quietly in the back of a classroom when I need to get away. Just being reminded of the simple basics of what we do can sometimes refresh my educator's soul.

Try rediscovering all the things you first enjoyed about your job—and try to do them more often! Do you love reading to classes? Do that more often. Do you love technology? Think of some ways to incorporate more technology into your job. Do you love working with families? I'm talking about the families that you can really make a difference with. Do you like home visits? I love home visits!

Let me tell you why I love home visits. (Random fun story here that I think some of you can relate too.) First, there are the positive home visits. Even though I don't go on those visits, those visits are to help families and give them practical parenting advice and activities. It's super rewarding mentally (maybe not so much monetarily, but that's for another book).

When you go to a student's home, they know you care. You may be visiting because they have been absent. You may take a student home from school for discipline or head lice. (WHOA!! I do not advise taking students with head lice home in your own vehicle. Have you ever had to treat head lice? There are school vehicles or the the school resource officer car you could use.)

Back to home visits. You can learn so much about a student by visiting his or her home. If your "why" is to help people and make a difference, after a home visit, you may then have four or five ways you can help and make a difference with that family over the course of the school year.

Then there are the home visits gone wrong. These are my favorite! They can be disheartening but quite humorous at the same time. We had a student who was going to miss the last couple days of school. The last few days of school are the best! I did not want him to miss it. Off we go: school resource officer, my counselor, and me. The disheartening part was the living conditions of the family. I can't even. The family moved not long after this visit.

However, watching my counselor get chased by chickens—in the mud, no less—made it quite rewarding. (I love you, Mrs. Woodall.) The fact that the family dog was named after her son was even more comical for both of us. The student's mom said he was "down by the pond, giggin' frogs." Off we tramped through the mud to the "pond." Once in the car on our way back to school with the student, we learned about his pet snakes he kept in the freezer.

The reason I tell you this story is for the humor. You must find the humor in some of the hardest situations. I'm not laughing at the family's situation; I am laughing at my counselor and me getting chased by chickens. Self-care includes being able to find the humor to be able to keep going. Back to school and onto the next challenge.

I mentioned my counselor, and that reminded me of the importance of connection. Not having an assistant principal, I have to rely on my counselor, my secretary, and my teachers for a lot of help. Whom do you rely on? Whom do you connect with at work in person? It's hard to have a "friend" as a leader, but there should be someone you can bounce ideas off of, share stories with, or even just eat lunch with. School dynamics are different everywhere, and it may be another principal or leader in your district. If you are the lone principal, social media has been life changing for me.

There is just something about reaching out to someone who can have an unbiased opinion or different lens from which to see. Amber and I met on Voxer. You would not be reading this book right now had it not been for social media. Twitter is where it all started for me. Jessica Johnson from Dodgeland Elementary School in Wisconsin calls me her Twitter godmother. (Not sure that's as endearing as she meant for it to be.)

While speaking around the country, Beth Houf, the pirate leader herself, has commented on and shared with the Facebook groups we started. Beth says these groups are the only redeeming quality of Facebook. She said she was almost ready to throw in the towel on Facebook.

Speaking of Facebook and self-care, those two things might not always go hand in hand. Do you sit and aimlessly scroll through Facebook? Me too. Be mindful of the images you're seeing. Do you struggle with comparisons? That Unfollow button exists for a reason, friends! Pinterest principal peer pressure is real. Don't allow your escape to be something that actually adds more pressure to your world! At the same time, Facebook groups can be awesome. I am not talking about the groups that are selling things but those groups about hobbies, pastimes, and passions. Name the niche, and there's a group for that! They're educationally relevant, inspiring, and many will just make you feel better about your world. Most of the time, I just click straight to the groups I'm in and see what's new.

Gratitude Journals

Every morning while waiting for my coffee to brew, I (Melinda) write down three things I am grateful for. I legit write them down in a small Happy Planner. At the end of the year, I will be able to go back and read through everything I was grateful for last year. God and family are non-negotiable. I am forever grateful for those two, and I don't write them every day.

Things I am grateful for:

- New makeup
- Snow days
- Our veterinarian
- My secretary
- Clean laundry (underwear and socks specifically)
- Coffee
- Cute fonts

This practice has changed my mindset more than any other habit I have started. This idea came from Brendan Bouchard's book, *High Performance Habits*. He talks about habit "triggers." Every time you do "x," it triggers "y." For me that is making coffee and writing down my gratitude for the day. The Happy Planner sits next to the coffee pot to make it quick and easy.

Positive Affirmations

Knowing that I am responsible for choosing my own personal weather, I have just recently started using positive affirmations in the morning. It's either that or worry and negative self-talk. This habit is triggered by my curling iron. (Sorry, guys. Maybe for the men reading this book, it can be shaving?) When I start using my curling iron, the positive affirmations begin:

I am smart.

I am pretty.

I got this.

Louise Hay, who is known as one of the founders of the self-help movement, shares that we have to retrain our thinking and speaking into positive patterns if we want to change our lives. Every thought you think and every word you speak is an affirmation. All of our self-talk, our internal dialogue, is a stream of affirmations. You're using affirmations every moment whether you know it or not. If that is true, don't you want to fill yourself with the most positive of thoughts?

> # Every thought you think and every word you speak is an affirmation.

Goal Setting

The struggle is real, people! I used to be terrible at this. Terrible. I set goals because it was "the thing to do." Lose weight, run a 5K, save money, and the list goes on. The aforementioned were actually as detailed as I ever got. I knew I wasn't going to achieve the goal. I could at least take part in unrealistic goal conversations with everyone else who was setting unattainable goals, right?

After four or five years of life-draining tragedies, I needed something to look forward to. I also needed to be a bit more positive. I realized my thoughts could own me, or I could own my thoughts. Our school recently started the Leader in Me initiative and practicing *The 7 Habits of Highly Effective People*. Life lessons were starting to fall into place. Here are the three that I chose. Notice how different they are from the typical goals I had always struggled to reach:

- Goal 1: Finish this book! Mark the due date to the publisher and, working back from that date, write for at least two hours every full day the girls are with their dad.

- Goal 2: Be positive. Use positive language at least three times a day. This was a public goal shared with my staff, and there are times when this goal is pretty comical. How many of your secretaries take the brunt of your venting? Amen! I have the world's greatest secretary. Ever. She puts up with a lot. During episodes of extreme stress and negative feedback, my strategy was to tell her how nice her hair looked. I'd take a deep breath, walk up to her desk, and say, "Your hair looks so nice today!" We would both crack up. I counted this as one of the three times I used positive language; my attitude changed, and I could easily find two more opportunities to use positive language. You have to do what you have to do.

- Goal 3: Decide upon and take action on what success will look like in the next ten years of my professional career. When will I retire? What will I do then?

Here's the thing about goals—setting them is the easiest part. It's the implementation that's difficult, but a detailed plan truly makes all the difference in the world! Are you wondering if I am going to mention exercise, massages, or taking naps as self-care strategies? Nope! You have to find what works for you when it comes to lifestyle changes or one-off self-care tactics. I can exercise and still be just as mad or stressed out after a good run as when I started. For me, self-care starts with improving my mindset.

Remembering to take care of yourself must be a priority, not something that you feel an additional level of stress about. Sometimes a conversation with a colleague-turned-friend will energize you. Sometimes you just need a nap. Learn to recognize the signs of stress that might trigger the need for self-care. The analogy of needing to put the oxygen mask on yourself before helping others has never been more relevant when you're leading adults who work with children. You all deserve to bring your very best selves to work each day!

Conclusion

It can be lonely at the top. It's a cliché for a reason. Never feel guilty for spending time doing the things that fill your bucket. I've found that even a thirty-minute chunk of something that makes me happy can calm my chaos. It doesn't have to be fancy or expensive. It can be something that I give to myself with no guilt. We push and push and support and support, and sometimes we need to step away and refresh. We all know we would give this same advice to a colleague or staff member who was feeling burned out. Be the one who takes your own advice. Self-care is important and can be the difference between an administrator on fire and an administrator fired.

Reflect on Self-Care

Leadership Treasure Hunt (Find This)

Find one self-care activity that you enjoy. It can be free, expensive, superfluous, or necessary. You get to decide.

Navigating the Seas (Think about This)

What are the signs that your tank is running on empty? Which colleagues and friends can help you see that it's time for a reset?

Charting the Course (Take Action)

Write your chosen activity on a sticky note and place it in your planner, next to your coffee pot, or on your bathroom mirror. It will serve as your visual reminder to yourself to take care of you!

Share your thoughts and ideas!
#LeadWithAppreciation

Bibliography

Pirate Motto Page

Ziglar, Zig. "Quotable Quotes." Goodreads. Publication date and/
or access date if available. goodreads.com/quotes/784099-
people-often-say-motivation-doesn-t-last-neither-does-
bathing-that-s-why.

Chapter 1

Flade, Peter, Jim Asplund, and Gwen Elliot. "Employees Who
Use Their Strengths Outperform Those Who Don't." Gallup.
October 8, 2015. gallup.com/workplace/236561/employees-
strengths-outperform-don.aspx.

Chapter 2

Rath, Tom. *Wellbeing: The Five Essential Elements*. New York, NY:
Gallup Press, 2010.

Whitaker, Todd. *What Great Principals Do Differently: Eighteen
Things That Matter Most*. New York, NY: Routledge, 2015.

Chapter 4

Arend, Matt. "Building School Culture - #SummerSelfieBingo."
My Thoughts . . . May Reflections . . . A Principal View
(blog). May 17, 2017. matthewarend.com/2017/05/27/
building-school-culture-summerselfiebingo/.

Travis, Jessica. "Tech Tips with Travis: Creating a Social Media Image." Jessica Travis Teaching (blog). July 4, 2018. jessicatravisteaching.com/tech-tips-with-travis-creating-a-social-media-image/.

Rath, Tom and Donald O. Clifton. *How Full Is Your Bucket?* New York, NY: Gallup Press, 2004.

Chapter 6

Achor, Shawn. "The Happiness Advantage: The Seven Principles of Positive Psychology that Fuel Success and Performance at Work." Shawn Achor. 2018. shawnachor.com/the-books/the-happiness-advantage/.

Chapman, Gary, and Paul White. *The 5 Languages of Appreciation in the Workplace: Empowering Organizations by Encouraging People.* Chicago: Northfield Publishing, 2011.

Chapter 11

Sahakian, Barbara and Jamie N. LaBuzetta. *Bad moves: How decision making goes wrong, and the ethics of smart drugs.* London: Oxford University Press. 2013.

MORE FROM
DAVE BURGESS
Consulting, inc.

Since 2012, DBCI has been publishing books that inspire and equip educators to be their best. For more information on our DBCI titles or to purchase bulk orders for your school, district, or book study, visit **DaveBurgessconsulting.com/DBCIbooks**.

More from the *Like a PIRATE*™ Series

Teach Like a PIRATE by Dave Burgess

eXPlore Like a Pirate by Michael Matera

Learn Like a Pirate by Paul Solarz

Play Like a Pirate by Quinn Rollins

Run Like a Pirate by Adam Welcome

Lead Like a PIRATE™ Series

Lead Like a PIRATE by Shelley Burgess and Beth Houf

Balance Like a Pirate by Jessica Cabeen, Jessica Johnson, and Sarah Johnson

Lead beyond Your Title by Nili Bartley

Lead with Culture by Jay Billy

Lead with Literacy by Mandy Ellis

Leadership & School Culture

Culturize by Jimmy Casas

Escaping the School Leader's Dunk Tank by Rebecca Coda
and Rick Jetter

From Teacher to Leader by Starr Sackstein

The Innovator's Mindset by George Couros

Kids Deserve It! by Todd Nesloney and Adam Welcome

Let Them Speak by Rebecca Coda and Rick Jetter

The Limitless School by Abe Hege and Adam Dovico

The Pepper Effect by Sean Gaillard

The Principled Principal by Jeffrey Zoul and Anthony McConnell

Relentless by Hamish Brewer

The Secret Solution by Todd Whitaker, Sam Miller, and
Ryan Donlan

Start. Right. Now. by Todd Whitaker, Jeffrey Zoul, and
Jimmy Casas

Stop. Right. Now. by Jimmy Casas and Jeffrey Zoul

They Call Me "Mr. De" by Frank DeAngelis

Unmapped Potential by Julie Hasson and Missy Lennard

Word Shift by Joy Kirr

Your School Rocks by Ryan McLane and Eric Lowe

Technology & Tools

50 Things You Can Do with Google Classroom by Alice Keeler
and Libbi Miller

50 Things to Go Further with Google Classroom by Alice Keeler
and Libbi Miller

140 Twitter Tips for Educators by Brad Currie, Billy Krakower,
and Scott Rocco

Block Breaker by Brian Aspinall

Code Breaker by Brian Aspinall

Google Apps for Littles by Christine Pinto and Alice Keeler

Master the Media by Julie Smith

Shake Up Learning by Kasey Bell

Social LEADia by Jennifer Casa-Todd

Teaching Math with Google Apps by Alice Keeler and Diana Herrington

Teachingland by Amanda Fox and Mary Ellen Weeks

Teaching Methods & Materials

All 4s and 5s by Andrew Sharos

Boredom Busters by Katie Powell

The Classroom Chef by John Stevens and Matt Vaudrey

Ditch That Homework by Matt Miller and Alice Keeler

Ditch That Textbook by Matt Miller

Don't Ditch That Tech by Matt Miller, Nate Ridgway, and Angelia Ridgway

EDrenaline Rush by John Meehan

Educated by Design by Michael Cohen, The Tech Rabbi

The EduProtocol Field Guide by Marlena Hebern and Jon Corippo

The EduProtocol Field Guide: Book 2 by Marlena Hebern and Jon Corippo

Instant Relevance by Denis Sheeran

LAUNCH by John Spencer and A.J. Juliani

Make Learning MAGICAL by Tisha Richmond

Pure Genius by Don Wettrick

The Revolution by Darren Ellwein and Derek McCoy

Shift This! by Joy Kirr

Spark Learning by Ramsey Musallam

Sparks in the Dark by Travis Crowder and Todd Nesloney

Table Talk Math by John Stevens

The Wild Card by Hope and Wade King

The Writing on the Classroom Wall by Steve Wyborney

Inspiration, Professional Growth & Personal Development

Be REAL by Tara Martin

Be the One for Kids by Ryan Sheehy

Creatively Productive by Lisa Johnson

Educational Eye Exam by Alicia Ray

The EduNinja Mindset by Jennifer Burdis

Empower Our Girls by Lynmara Colón and Adam Welcome

The Four O'Clock Faculty by Rich Czyz

How Much Water Do We Have? by Pete and Kris Nunweiler

P Is for Pirate by Dave and Shelley Burgess

A Passion for Kindness by Tamara Letter

The Path to Serendipity by Allyson Apsey

Sanctuaries by Dan Tricarico

The SECRET SAUCE by Rich Czyz

Shattering the Perfect Teacher Myth by Aaron Hogan

Stories from Webb by Todd Nesloney

Talk to Me by Kim Bearden

Teach Me, Teacher by Jacob Chastain

Through the Lens of Serendipity by Allyson Apsey

The Zen Teacher by Dan Tricarico

Children's Books

Beyond Us by Aaron Polansky

Dolphins in Trees by Aaron Polansky

I Want to Be a Lot by Ashley Savage

The Princes of Serendip by Allyson Apsey

Zom-Be a Design Thinker by Amanda Fox

LEAD WITH APPRECIATION AT YOUR SCHOOL!

Invite Amber Teamann or Melinda Miller to your next school or district professional development event!

Amber Teamann

Through her experiences as a teacher, a technology facilitator, and an administrator, Amber has a wide breadth of experiences. From technology roll-outs to integrating a cultural change, authentic experiences have opened a number of possibilities. From a think tank with the Board of Education to consulting with administrators one-on-one, she has had the privilege to speak and present at a variety of conferences, school districts, events, and beyond. Amber speaks on a variety of topics that focus on empowering administrators, teachers, and students in the workplace, leadership, technology integration, innovation, literacy, and more! She is more than happy to tailor her offerings below to meet the needs of your participants or any audience, so please do not hesitate to contact her with any questions.

Keynotes and Speaking Topics

- Lead with Appreciation
- Changing the Way We Think About Leadership
- Digital Leadership & Why it Matters
- School Culture: Leading in a Critical Time
- Get off your Admin Island!
- Empowering Teacher Growth and Leadership
- Building a Collaborative Culture Within Your School
- Principal Productivity

- Using Social Media in Schools to Connect with Your Community and Beyond

Break-Out Sessions

Amber has a number of presentations on social media, innovation in the classroom and campus, empowering teacher leadership, tech integration, and principal productivity. Many of her break-out sessions below can be tailored to fit the depth and breadth needed for a longer speaking engagement or a shorter break-our session. Here are some options below that can also be modified to fit your learners:

- Social Media and the Principal's Office
- PLC: Plug & Play
- Using Twitter to Boost your Instructional Leadership
- Work Smarter, not Harder! Leveraging Talents in your School
- How Do We Leverage Our Personal Talents in Schools? (Leading with your strengths!)
- Earth Shaking Moves for Integration Success
- Tech Integration—What does it mean and how do we get there?
- Twitter 101 for Principals
- Using Instagram in the Classroom
- Take Charge of your Professional Growth
- Empowering Students and Families Using Social Media
- Digital Storytelling in the Classroom
- DRA, gone Digital!
- Digital Citizenship and Leadership for Students and Staff
- Connecting to Global Classrooms
- Technology as a Tool, Not a Process
- Build Engaging PD for Teachers (Workshop Model)

If you're ready to level up your event with Amber, email her at: amberteamann@gmail.com.

Melinda Miller

As a twenty-six-year veteran educator, Melinda brings a wide variety of experience to the table. From coaching experiences to classroom experience to directing multiple district programs, she brings wisdom from multiple perspectives. Through her presentations at national, state, local and online conferences, Melinda has positively impacted thousands of school leaders with her wisdom and sense of humor. She doesn't hold back. Her passion and honesty are filtered through the lens of humor and grace.

Keynotes and Speaking Topics

- Lead with Appreciation
- Leadership in the Digital Wild
- Leveling Up Your School Culture
- Empowering Teacher Leaders
- Principal Productivity
- Using Social Media in Schools to Connect with Your Community and Beyond

Presentation Topics

- Using Social Media as a Window Into Your School
- Staff Communication: Tips, Tricks, and Tools to Communicate Effectively with Your Staff
- Work Smarter, not Harder! Productivity Tips and Tools for Administrators
- Google Take the Wheel: Getting the most from your Google tools
- Flipped Faculty Meetings
- Twitter 101 for Principals
- Instagram and Facebook Stories to Maximize Your Message

- Email Strategies for Administrators: How to get parents and teachers to look forward to your emails
- Lessons Learned from Students On Social Media
- Secretaryella: Myths and legends of working in a school office and how to leverage your time at work
- #EDCamp Model: Allowing staff to personalize their Professional Development

Inquire about Melinda's online and in-person presentations at mmiller7571@gmail.com.

About the Authors

Amber Teamann is the proud principal of Whitt Elementary in Wylie ISD in Wylie, Texas. During her educational career, Amber's comprehensive understanding of student learning has resulted in a successful blend of technology and teaching. From a fourth-grade teacher at a public school technology center to her role as a Title I  technology facilitator responsible for seventeen campuses, Amber has helped students and staff navigate their digital abilities and responsibilities. She transformed the way information is shared in one of the largest school districts in Texas by piloting a communication initiative that launched Twitter and led to 100 percent campus participation. Through her campus-level leadership, she has helped initiate classroom change district wide, empowering teachers at all levels through digital initiatives.

Amber has received numerous awards, including Regional Assistant Principal of the Year and a Principal of the Year engagement award. She recently was recognized as the Dallas Down Syndrome Educator of the Year for her work with inclusivity on her campus. TCEA honored her as a state finalist for Administrator of the Year. She also partnered with George Couros to develop and curate leadership with the "School Admin Virtual Mentoring Project," which connected more than 4000 educators worldwide in a digital space that nurtured and cultivated leadership. She was a contributing author for Education Write Now on changing the way people think about leadership. Through her state organization, TEPSA, she has shared in numerous webinars, articles, and conferences with administrators at all levels.

Amber has also cocreated a space on Facebook for principals by principals that shares staff appreciation and motivation ideas and tips and tricks to ensure the well-being of campus staff. With over 5000 members, it has become a collaborative space where administrators are able to connect, be renewed, and feel as if taking care of their people is a FUN and easy thing to do. A second group focuses on Principal Productivity. Through these groups, in 2019, Amber (with Melinda) launched "The Leadership Vault," a subscription-based service to support and empower school leaders.

Having delivered keynote presentations at several events, she is passionate about inspiring innovation through her experiences and impetus for student success in a digitally full world. Amber speaks nationally at educational conferences, including the 2016 Digital Learning Day in conjunction with the U.S. Department of Education in Washington, D.C. She also developed and led the inaugural Region X Digital Fluency Academy for Administrators, supporting her favorite quote, "The smartest person in the room is the room." Amber knows we can all be better together and strives to make every day the very best it can be for each member of her staff and students.

When she isn't tweeting, watching sports, or principal-ing, she is chasing around her fireman husband and two daughters. They keep her on her toes at all times!

Melinda Miller has been an

education professional for more than twenty-five years. She has served The Willard School district for all twenty-five of those years as an elementary teacher, junior high school basketball coach, high school track coach, and for the last fifteen years, proud principal of Willard East Elementary. During her tenure  as an elementary school principal, she has also served on the local and state levels of the Missouri Association of Elementary School Principals.

In 2008 Melinda was named Southwest Missouri New Principal of the Year. In 2010 she was selected as one of only fifty administrators across the nation to attend the Google Certified Administrator Academy in San Antonio, Texas. Melinda was then selected in 2015 as the Southwest Missouri Distinguished Principal.

Melinda's most passionate about supporting and growing teachers who in turn create innovative and relationship based classrooms. Another passion of hers is connecting with and helping other principals around the globe. Through podcasts, Facebook groups, blogs, and attending state and national conferences, Melinda has created a community of principals working together to uplift and appreciate teachers and staff.

When not supporting principals, teachers, and students, Melinda is the chauffeur and sports agent to her two preteen daughters, Alyson and Cassidy.